Eustacia Cutler

T0160977

A Thorn in My Pocket

Temple Grandin's Mother
Tells the Family Story

Future Horizons, Inc.

A Thorn in My Pocket

All marketing and publishing rights guaranteed to
and reserved by

FUTURE HORIZONS

817-277-0727
817-277-2270 (fax)
E-mail: info@FHautism.com
www.FHautism.com

ISBN: 978-1-941765-40-1

For My Children

Think of me as your future. I am where you will be many years from now, when you know how it all played out and "what will be" has turned into "what was."

And you will have come to terms with it, not perhaps in the way you thought you would, but you'll no longer feel trapped in a morass of angst and guilt. You will have resolved your child's future and your own. You'll know you've given full measure and the measure you've given has never been pointless.

I offer you my story as a promise of that, an overall insight to carry with you as a talisman. And I promise that in the future, to your surprise, your dreams will have changed, and changed you.

I know that's not what you want.

What you want is a real talisman, a magic something you think I conjured up to coax Temple into joining life as you hope your child will.

There was no magic, there was just doing the best I could. That's the point, that's the talisman.

And never letting go of hope.

~Eustacia

Any beetle can live a flawless, impeccable life, infallible in the business of procreating beetles. Not us: we are not necessarily good at anything in particular except language and using this we tend to get things wrong. It's built into our genes to veer off from the point; somehow we have been selected in evolution for our gift of ambiguity...

...We do not understand why we make music, or dance, or write poems...We are bewildered, especially in this century, by the pervasive latency of love...

Lewis Thomas, M.D.
Chancellor, Memorial Sloan
Kettering Cancer Center, NYC

1980 Harvard Phi Beta Kappa Oration:
"On The Uncertainty of Science," *Harvard Magazine*, 1980

Acknowledgements

My gratitude goes first to my four children. Uniquely talented, they have each traveled an individual path, each triumphed over obstacles, each realized fulfillment.

A special thanks to Temple for being Temple, also for persuading me to join her on the autism lecture circuit, a road to which she's deeply committed. Special thanks to Wayne Gilpin, president of Future Horizons, for inviting me to lecture for him and for supporting me, not only in the lectures but in the production of this book.

The first inkling for the book came from friend and New York agent, Fifi Oscard, of Fifi Oscard Agency, Inc., who, on hearing my story, said, "You must write this."

Michael Denneny, New York freelance editor, has been invaluable in helping me weave a multitude of lectures into a coherent whole. Lyn Dunsavage, Future Horizons editor, has contributed her astute eye and judgment. Victoria Ulmer, Editorial Coordinator, has carried off a load of publication details with good nature and amazing dispatch. Layout artist Matt Mitchell has transformed the manuscript into a book.

Professional friends who've advised me through various drafts are Sue Lawless, Lois Bianchi, Beulah Robinson, and Dorothy Emmerson.

Doctors who've taken the time to educate me personally are Eric Hollander, M.D., Mt. Sinai; Nancy Minshew, M.D., Professor of Psychiatry and Neurology and head of the Autism Project at the University of Pittsburgh Medical Center; David E. Reiser, M.D., psychatrist/psychoanalyst of Salt Lake City; Barry Gordon,

M.D., Ph.D., professor of neurology and cognitive science, founder of the Memory Clinic, holder of an endowed chair to study the treatment of brain disorders at John Hopkins Medical Institutions, Baltimore, MD.; Eveyn Davis, M.D., Behavioral Development Pediatrician, Dept. Of Pediatrics, Dept. of Child/Adolescent Psychiatry, Harlem Hospital Center, Columbia College of Physicians and Surgeons, New York, NY; William M. McMahon, M.D., Principal Investigator, Tourette Research Dept., The University of Utah, Salt Lake City, UT.

Autism Center Directors who've encouraged and educated me are Gary Mesibov, Ph.D., Director of TEACCH, Chapel Hill, NC; Raymond B. White, Chief Operating Officer, and Marilyn Hoyson, Ph.D., Director of The Watson Institute, Sewickly, PA; Catherine Lord, Ph.D., Director of University of Michigan Autism and Communication Disorder Center, Ann Arbor, MI; Ruth Christ Sullivan, Ph.D., President of Autism Services Center, Huntington, WV; Bernard Rimland, Ph.D., Director of Autism Research Institute, San Diego, CA.

I think with gratitude of therapists Rebecca Klaw at Pressley Ridge School, Pittsburgh, PA; Barbara Hanft of Silver Spring, MD, Nancy Reiser of Salt Lake City, UT, and Laura Schreibman of San Diego, CA.

A special thanks to Clara Claiborne Park, author of *The Seige* and *Exiting Nirvana* for her insight, and to Joyce Douglas for helping me to negotiate Pittsburgh's agencies.

Table of Contents

Prologue

An image haunts me.

Temple, just turned three, is lying in a hospital bed. A nurse leans over her, gluing wires to her scalp.

Terrified, Temple struggles and screams. I try to soothe her—and myself—telling her it won't hurt, that it's only wires, telling myself to practice distancing as the medics do. Yes, just withdraw into that safe place where everything is reduced to an interesting research study, a laboratory haven unconnected to feeling.

But Temple's haven is dangerous, her brain has trapped her in an icy limbo where she must live each day denied response. I hold onto her hand and vow I won't let her freeze to death in that tempting snowdrift, so I, too, mustn't go there or we'll both freeze.

Temple stops her thrashing and grows sleepy. The nurse has given her a sedative, she assures me it won't affect the reading. Watching Temple fade off, I whisper scraps of Keats.

My heart aches, and a drowsy numbness pains
My sense, as though of hemlock I had drunk.

Finally, the medication takes effect. Temple falls into a deep hospital swoon. The electroencephalogram is ready to register her living brain waves.

Fifty-five years from that moment when her prognosis lay in question, Temple will be known the world over for her miraculous triumph over autism. My story is of her first young journey, from 1947, when she was born, to 1962 when, at fourteen, she went away to a special boarding school. It's also her father's story. Both stories have great holes in them where I've lost hunks of the past through timidity and denial. Perhaps in the process of writing, I'll be able to find them and perhaps I won't and perhaps that's just as well. There must be a reason for repression.

There are also hunks missing because my other three children have asked to be omitted from this tale, which says worlds about their childhood or lack of it. While trying to help Temple, I left them in the dark. Their innocence lost, they had to be braver and more generous than children should have to be. Temple and Daddy were the stars—the siblings and I, minor constellations circling uneasily around them. In spite of it, the siblings have grown up to be wise and unique, and I've endeavored to honor the spirit of their request.

I was young when Temple was born, both in years and experience. I soon found out that, if I was going to help her—or any of us—I'd have to put away my baby terror and grapple with whatever each day brought. So, in effect, the story is also that of my own young awakening and growth: a classic bildungsroman, if you will.

How did I come to write it?

A few years ago, Temple—now a full fledged college professor with a second career designing cattle handling equipment, and a third career as star lecturer on the autism circuit—asked me if I would join her in lecturing.

I've arrived late to this task. Putting the years into words for an audience hasn't been easy, so I've taken my cue from Robert Frost who said, "I teach to find kindred spirits, to comfort them and myself." In the process of that, I've learned how the parents of autistic children suffer from a loss of their own sense of self. We all know that a baby needs a mother to know she's a baby, but, equally true, a mother needs a baby to know she's a mother.

When those first infant/mother responses can't grow, a whole family identity is thrown out of kilter. I understand that far better now, from the vantage point of years, than I could when I was young. I understand, too, how much parents long to be good parents. The purpose of my lectures is to find them and comfort them in their never ending battle with autism.

"Think of me as your future," I tell them. "I am where you will be many years from now, when you know how it all played out, when 'what will be' has turned into 'what was,' and you will have come to terms with it."

"Perhaps not in the way you thought you would, but you'll no longer feel trapped in a morass of angst and guilt. You will have resolved your child's future and your own. You'll know you've given full measure, and the measure you've given has never been pointless."

"I offer you my story as a promise of that: an overall insight to carry with you as a talisman. And I promise that, in the future, to your surprise, your dreams will have changed and changed you."

"I know that's not what you want."

"What you want is a real talisman, a magic something you think I conjured up to coax Temple into joining life, as you hope your child will. There was no magic; there was just doing the best I could. That's the point; that's the talisman."

Theodore Morrison, who knew Robert Frost well, said that Frost also came late to lecturing and was never entirely at ease with it.

"I always carry something in my pocket I can touch when I'm talking," he told Morrison, "so I'll remember who I am. Lately it's been a thorn."

A Thorn in
My Pocket

Chapter 1

And Baby Makes Three

August 29, 1947. Temple isn't born; she's induced. As is the present medical custom, I'm drugged almost out of consciousness, and my waters ruptured by a nurse. I thrash about for hours in an artificial labor and finally pass out cold. The doctor cuts me open from the vagina to the anus, takes the baby, and stitches me back together like a Christmas goose. Hours later, I regain enough consciousness to see my husband Dick hovering over the bed with a huge bunch of yellow chrysanthemums and magnolia leaves.

"What did I have?"

"You had a girl."

"Can I see her?"

The nurse leaps in. "The baby can't be exhibited until the next feeding." The baby is her property, sealed off in a nursery behind a glass wall where I can't hear her cry. "Because," the nurse explains, "we have to establish a schedule. The baby must learn to cry alone until it's feeding time."

I fall back into a stupor. By the time I come to again, Dick has gone, and it's long past the 9:30 feeding time. The nurse says it's

1

too late to make an exception, I'll have to wait till morning to see my baby.

"After all, I can't be running her up and down the corridor, exposing her to possible germs."

That night I'm hit by an attack of grinding afterbirth pains. No one's told me about afterbirth pains, and in the druggy dark, I keep having the same nightmare over and over: I'm giving birth to another baby, and there's no one to help me.

A few days later, my milk comes in and I swell up to the size of two croquet balls. The nurse gives my nipples a painful pinch.

"You can't nurse," she announces. "You have inverted nipples."

Inverted? I look down. My nipples have disappeared into the veined agony of two immense, cement udders.

"Why do you want to nurse your baby anyway? Nobody does that anymore. Besides, we wouldn't bring the baby out to you for the 2:00 a.m. feeding. What's the point? The nurse is up. The baby's up. The mother's up. You need your sleep."

She thrusts the baby's mouth up against my throbbing breast. The baby turns her cheek to my nipple, her tiny mouth makes sucking motions. My heart leaps. Milk dribbles out of me; the baby tastes it and turns her cheek to me again. I dribble some more. The baby's brand new pink mouth, only days old, roots about in vain, then she lets out "lah! lah!" screams of frustration. Incessant, rhythmic. I didn't know that's how new babies cry. Her upper lip curls back to show the tiny pink kitten-membrane attached miraculously to her upper gum. Somewhere inside that gum are little seeds of teeth. Her tongue curls back, the shape of a heart, the shape of every cartoon heart tongue. Her eyes shut tight, nothing visible but a spiky fringe of tiny lashes against her cheek, now red as my breast. She screams, milk pours out of me. The milk I want so much to give her; it's there and it's not there.

The frustration exhausts us both. Love doesn't cut it, and the nurse takes the baby away.

Later in the morning, the doctor gives orders for me to be pumped. The nurse makes a face, brings the pump, clamps it on me and sets it going. Pain! Unimaginable pain!

"That's because you're already giving too much milk," she says. "With the pump, you'll give even more, so the pain will be worse."

Perhaps the nurse is right.

"Do you want me to take the pump away?"

I nod. I give up. She takes the pump away.

The next day, miraculously, I have nipples. They work, and the baby can suckle, but the nipples are now ulcerated. The nurse applies some kind of stinging salve. The baby screams at the taste of it—heartbreaking screams. I would do anything to assuage her infant grief. Then, surprise: hunger wins out and the baby is feeding. I have milk in abundance for her, but the pull of her suck on my ulcerated nipples is making the ulcers worse.

Meanwhile, in the time between feedings, a ritual social hour takes place, and a steady stream of visitors parade into my room. Reared to social obligation, I array myself in a silver gray negligee with ruffles down the front and receive my guests, hoping my milk won't leak through the crepe de Chine. My baby, too, has her social hour. Sealed in her germ-free nursery, she is wheeled up to an observation window for visitor inspection.

At last the required ten days are up. The hospital nurse brings in my baby and dresses her in the tiny infant clothes I've brought with me from a Best & Co. layette*, along with an infant sweater I've knitted, and a receiving blanket knit by my mother. Elated, I dress myself. The ulcers have improved. I'm ready for our new life together.

---

* "Layette" is an old-fashioned term for a complete baby outfit: sheets, blankets, shirts, nighties, etc. Best & Co. used to pack it all in a special pink-ribboned box. If you had twins, Best's would give you a second layette for free.

There's a knock at the door. It's the practical nurse who has been hired to go home with me for the customary six weeks. We all ride down in the elevator together: Dick, the hospital nurse carrying the baby, the practical nurse, and me in a wheelchair. I'm not allowed to stand on my own until out the hospital door. The hospital nurse carries the baby to the door, then hands her to me. At last she's mine. But no, the practical nurse steps forward.

"The home nurse carries the new baby," she announces, sweeping her from my arms.

I ride in the front seat with Dick, cradling the last of the fading chrysanthemums and magnolia leaves. The home nurse rides in back, cradling my baby. I keep turning around to look at her, but she's fast asleep, oblivious to the arms that hold her.

Finally we're home, but home looks a bit strange. I'm allowed to walk up the one flight of stairs to my bedroom. Only once a day will I be allowed to walk the stairs. That, too, is part of the ritual: no stairs for six weeks. We put the baby in the bassinet borrowed from my sister-in-law. Weeks earlier, I've washed and pressed its quilted silk lining, sewn on new tie ribbons, papered the nursery wall in pale blue with pink lilacs. The bureau I've painted white. Then, in a flight of fancy, I've painted the drawers with a flourish of tumbling blue and pink baby blocks, a letter on each block, spelling out "Baby Grandin." In the weeks before the birth, I've opened the drawers over and over, to arrange and rearrange the perfect little Best and Co. layette. I know every shift, blanket and garment by heart, but now they all look insignificant. Feeling let down, I watch the nurse put the baby in the bassinet; then Dick puts me into bed.

Finally, after much fussing and ceremony, the home nurse brings Temple in to me for her first feeding. She sucks. Nothing happens. She lets go, bleats her little "lah, lah," roots around for a better hold, sucks again, lets go, and cries in earnest. Something's wrong.

"We need formula," the nurse says.

4

"Why?"

"Your milk is gone."

I look down, I touch my breasts. They're flaccid.

It's long after business hours, so the local drug store is closed. Dick makes an emergency call to the owner. Together, he and the owner go to the drug store. The owner unlocks the door, and sells Dick the baby formula. Dick brings it home in a fury; the nurse heats it, puts it in a sterilized bottle, comes up to the bedroom, takes the screaming baby from me and departs, leaving me empty-armed. I look at Dick.

"Why can't I feed her the formula?"

Dick's mouth goes tight: "We wouldn't have this problem if you'd listened to the nurse at the hospital."

I lie there feeling useless and ashamed, Dick's angry words washing over me. The baby. The baby. When will she be *my* baby?

The next day, the home nurse, warning me about germs, shows me how to make a sterile formula. She feeds the baby; I watch. She shows me how to give the baby a bath. She bathes the baby; I watch. She shows me how to wash the baby blankets. She watches; I wash.

Finally, the six weeks are over and she leaves. I curl up alone with Temple. She's mine, mine. Yes, but she doesn't seem to care, and I'm not sure how to win her over. She's too quiet. She sleeps a great deal. Too much, perhaps? I don't know. Mother and baby, we don't either of us know.

Not an auspicious beginning.

Was that the beginning? I'm not sure. When did Temple take on her strangeness? With the men off fighting World War II, few babies have been born, so how would I, who've never even held a baby, know whether or not she's strange? Ashamed of my disloyalty, I let my qualms slip into the darkness. Temple and I go our separate ways—she into oversleeping, I into polishing silver for the coming housewarming party.

Still, there are moments in those early months, occasions at other houses where other mothers dress their babies in pretty outfits and play patty-cake, jig their babies up and down, show them off, dandle them, coax them into gurgling grins. Other mothers' babies snatch at earrings and jacket buttons. Drooling and chuckling, they grab fistfuls of their mothers' hair and try to stuff them in their mouths. Temple puts nothing in her mouth, not even her thumb.

I try dressing her up, but it feels odd. She looks pretty, but no patty-cake for her, thank you; no grabbing for my hair. I write off dandling and games to indulgence. I've been raised to think one shouldn't indulge one's baby, and my baby seems to understand this better than I do. I'm too green to admit, even to myself, that her indifference makes me feel trivial and snubbed.

The qualms return. I recall a baby doll I'd had as a child; how I'd bathed it and dressed it and put it to sleep on a little footstool I'd made up into a dolly bed, how I'd chosen to ignore what my doll was missing: that the puppy had chewed off its dimpled rubber fingers. My grandmother had sewn up the holes, so the hands looked almost whole if you didn't notice the knots of gray cotton thread. Not noticing. Was it an old trick?

Summer comes. I take Temple to the new swimming pool at the Dedham Polo Club and watch to see what the other mothers do. Since the wading pool is still being built, they put their toddlers into big orange life jackets and float with them in the shallow end of the grown-up pool. I copy them, and Temple, floating waist high in her jacket, seems almost to enjoy it.

In August, we go to the Vineyard. On a calm, waveless day on South Beach I put the life jacket on her again. We float together on the gentle swell, I standing waist deep, Temple riding waist high in her orange life jacket. I should have known better, should have known that South Beach, even on a calm day, was no swimming pool. A sudden swell lifts her out of my arms. I grab for her; the swell carries her sideways away from me. Frantic, screaming, I try to run to her in the water, but it's like dream running: I make no headway. Each time I grab for her, she slips further sideways, no deeper, no shallower, bobbing like a Halloween apple just out of my reach. A man hears my yells, sees what's happening, scrambles ashore, runs down the beach, dives into the water and catches her as she floats toward him on the current. Unconcerned, Temple accepts his rescue.

How could I have been so careless? How could I take the sea for granted? What if the man hadn't heard me, hadn't thought to get out of the water, run down the beach and catch her floating toward him on the current? Why hadn't I thought of that instead of yelling and churning and getting nowhere? But that would have meant abandoning her.

It will be years before I can look at an orange life jacket without the recollection returning to me in sick waves. And even more years before I can think beyond my long ago panic to puzzle over Temple's lack of response that gray day on South Beach, to see her lack as a symptom of what was to come. I can understand her enjoying bobbing in the sea and not being aware of the danger. Any child might do that. But when we became separated—a moment when most toddlers would have let out a howl—she had no response. Nor did she respond, good or bad, to being rescued by a stranger, even when the stranger handed her tenderly back to me. Through all of it, she seemed neither happy nor unhappy.

Was that the beginning? Is that when I began to pray, "Give her back to me"? Why the odd phrase "Give her back," as if she'd been taken away from me to somewhere quite far off?

Or did it all begin long before Temple was born, back when my soft gelatin self was first set out on the windowsill to stiffen in its tin mold?

I grew up in Springfield, Massachusetts in the middle of the Depression. I watched men scrounge in trashcans for something to eat, watched them sell pencils to my mother at the front door. My mother always offered them a meal.

When war came, my father joined the War Production Board, and we moved to Cambridge. By that time I was in boarding school in the Berkshires; the trains carrying us home for Christmas vacation were hours late and jammed with soldiers. We sat on our suitcases and flirted with them. Shoes were rationed along with butter, meat and sugar. Silk and rubber didn't exist. We resoled our sneakers with some kind of tarry substitute we spread on with a kitchen knife and hoped it would stick. Harvard was turned into a naval training post, and Radcliffe was put to training WAVES. Both groups marched through Harvard Square singing as they swung their arms.

In the middle of the war Winston Churchill made a secret visit to this country to urge us not to lose heart. As word went round that he was coming to Harvard, we wangled passes and crowded into the Harvard Yard. Squeezed together on the top steps of Widener Library, we craned our necks and, there across the Yard, on the steps of Memorial Chapel—that chapel built to honor the Harvard men who'd died in WWI—stood Winston Churchill, his bald head shining in the sunlight, his words from the Church of England Litany rolling out to us from the speakers attached to the trees.

"Till we have beat down Satan under our feet..."

The Yard was solid with rows of Navy men in dress uniform, their white hats like so many peppermints. We sang "God Save the King"—it was a king then—and "The Star Spangled Banner."

In June, 1944, when the war was at its peak, Dick Grandin and I met at the Boston Debutante Cotillion. I was seventeen, twenty-four hours out of a girls' boarding school, and he was an officer in the tank corps, on leave before being sent overseas. It was his thirtieth birthday, and he looked like Gary Cooper.

My father, in a rare moment of obstinacy, had refused to attend the Cotillion and present me to society. So Dick's older sister, who was giving a dinner in my honor, suggested Dick for the job. One look at him and my mortification over my father's betrayal turned to enchantment. Dick took my arm, escorted me down the red carpeted stairs, and the rest of the evening was a dizzying whirl of satin and uniforms and flashing photographers. The next morning our picture was on the society page. Topping that came three ecstatic days of telephone calls, flowers, and girl-friend envy. Dick then departed for duty overseas, where he announced by mail that he planned to marry me.

He returned after V-E Day, on leave before being shipped to California and the Pacific. On the warm summer night of his return we drove along the Charles River while he told me what had happened to his army commission and his tank unit during the Battle of the Bulge.

"I want you to know the story because that's who I am."

It was during the worst of the Battle of the Bulge. Dick was a 1st lieutenant in the tanks, attached to a reconnaissance group exploring the winter darkness to see if a unit advance was feasible or suicidal. In the process, he realized that the colonel above him was causing fifty percent of the casualties by commanding unit advances that were indeed suicidal.

Going over the colonel's head, Dick reported to the higher-ups that the colonel didn't know what he was doing. He, a lst lieutenant, planned to make an official report against the colonel. According to Dick, the higher-ups were sympathetic about the casualties but adamant about an official report. Perhaps they were worried about morale, perhaps the horror was too chaotic to assess, or perhaps they were under even higher orders. General Patton was known as "Old Blood and Guts."

The higher-ups thanked Dick and told him they would move the colonel to another war zone. However, they warned him that if he did make an official charge, the colonel's record would be kept under wraps and Dick would be moved to another tank unit. In addition, he would have to forfeit his advancement from lst lieutenant to major. Even in the face of that, Dick still insisted on an official report and had immediately been sent to another tank unit, never to fight again with the only unit buddies he'd known.

Was Dick's charge an act of ethical bravery? I thought so then. It seemed courageous and noble, and I adored him for it. To undertake reconnaissance in the midst of the Battle of the Bulge was in itself heroic—the stuff of John Wayne movies, and my schoolgirl head was full of movies. Today I'm not so sure. Knowing Dick, I'm certain he produced rules and numbers; otherwise the higher-ups would never have taken him seriously enough to move the colonel to another war zone. Why hadn't that sufficed? War calls for courage, resourcefulness, and total obedience. Dick must have known any higher war command would override his personal opinion.

"I want you to know the story because that's who I am."

Did that mean, "I want you to think of me as a hero, even though I may have done the wrong thing"? Or was he saying, "If you're going to marry me, know that when I make a decision, whether you think it's right or wrong, my decision stands"? Was he acknowledging a foolish rigidity, but as he recalled the scene, found himself, once again, unable to stop insisting that he was right?

Or was he merely explaining why he'd come home with a new unit number on his red, blue, and yellow tank triangle and still only the silver bars of a 1st lieutenant?

What neither Dick nor I knew on that warm summer night was that Dick's glory days were behind him.

At Harvard he'd been among the dashing clubmen who lived outside the dorms in what was called a "rat house," a separate rented house with a man servant. One of the rat-housers was Johnny Roosevelt who invited them all to Sunday night supper at the White House. Mrs. Roosevelt scrambled eggs for them in a silver chafing dish brought in by the maid and lighted ceremoniously. After supper, Gerswhin played them "Rhapsody in Blue."

Graduation came and after it more glory. Dick joined the 101st Cavalry in New York, the famous Squadron A. Squadron A men played polo in the old Armory, polished their riding boots, and dated Brenda Diana Duff Frazier, "the ultimate debutante"*. Some of the men even had the squadron emblem tattooed on a bicep; all of them had nicknames. Dick was called "Sticky Dick."

Then came WWII. Cavalry units became tank units, and the glory of Squadron A was forgotten.

In August, 1945, the war ended. General Patton was driven through Harvard Square, standing tall in an open jeep, his khaki helmet varnished till it gleamed like Churchill's dome. Glory was in the air again, but it had changed; it held no place now for social princelings. Yet the Squadron A men would go on calling each other by nickname the rest of their lives. And somewhere along in the years, one of them would say to me, "We always

---

* Gardner Botsford, *A Life of Privilege, Mostly*. St. Martin's Press. NY 2003. Botsford was a member of Squadron A.

knew Sticky Dick was crazy."

*

March 1946. My mother loved the world of Jane Austen. During my engagement to Dick, she glowed like Mrs. Bennet in *Pride and Prejudice;* her daughter was making a good marriage. She had the wedding invitations engraved on the best vellum and addressed them all herself. No, I could not touch them. Each invitation must be free of smudge, the visible proof of my mother's adroit social management.

The wedding presents arrived in white boxes. My mother helped me unwrap them: crystal, silver, and china. She laid them all lovingly on the dining room table, set off by her best white damask, and invited her friends in to see "the loot."

The night before the wedding, I was removed early from my bridal dinner, lest I be fatigued for the ceremony on the morrow. The same went for the next day luncheon given in my honor. I was to have sandwiches at home with my mother and her best friend and then to nap. Again, the fatigue factor. After the nap I was dressed two hours early in bridal finery, handed a bridal bouquet and told to pose for the photographer, who twisted me first one way and then another, moving the bouquet first to one side and then the other. The sitting pose presented problems: lots of satin to arrange so the dress wouldn't crease. My mother wanted a picture of herself in her wedding finery leaning over me, caressing my bouquet.

The wedding ceremony blended in somehow with the wedding reception line. Lots of hands to shake. A few friends from the Harvard Dramat came and were properly awed by the formality of shaking hands with me and mumbling appropriate words of congratulation.

Finally it was all over. I and the presents and the social glory departed from my mother's life. When she came to and realized the extent of her loss, she took small revenge by frowning on any purchase I made in my new role as a married woman, particularly one she could construe as "frivolous."

The first disapproval came with my purchase of a crystal hedgehog. She saw it on my mantel and drew in her breath.

"You bought yourself a crystal ornament? I never gave in to such an indulgence in my life!"

"The cleaning woman called in sick." I was desperate to justify my frivolity. "I cleaned the house myself and spent the cleaning money on the hedgehog."

My father, who was usually meek, came to my defense. "Mary, dear lamb,"—an endearment he used when he wanted to soothe my mother's ruffled feathers—"you must admit we spend a great deal of money on cleaning." My mother yielded not an inch.

I loved the crystal hedgehog and treasure it to this day, but as soon as my mother left, I hid it, as I was to hide so many pieces of my life.

Years later, when I learned how inherited traits ride on the DNA strands, I'd wonder if they added as much freight as my mother's long-ago label of "feckless indulgence."

Fear of her label spilled over into buying infant toys for Temple. The displays in toy stores were scant. The country was still tooling up after WWII. I stared at what little there was—a few cuddly bears good for nothing but a hug, clown dolls with big eyes, and a clear plastic ball with bright fish swimming inside. I stared and worried. Better not buy. Who knows where it could lead?

It took me nearly two years to get over the anxiety. It happened when I first brought Temple to the Judge Baker Guidance Clinic in Boston's Children's Hospital. But I'm getting ahead of myself.

*

May 1949. My second child is born, and I've carried her home myself. Again, a baby nurse has been hired, first to take care of Temple while I've been in the hospital, and then to help with the new baby.

The day is sunny and perfect. Temple and I are playing in the sandbox at the edge of the field behind our house. With us are my close friend, Veevee, and her little girl, Ceelie, a few months older than Temple. Temple is twenty-one months old now.

Ceelie fills her pail with sand and wets it down with the watering can. Chattering to herself, looking to us for praise, she begins turning out mud pies with a plastic mold. Mute, lost in her own private world, Temple gathers up handfuls of sand and watches the sand dribble slowly through her fingers. Over and over, unmoved by the praise we heap on Ceelie or the encouragement we offer to her—"Shall we make a patty-cake? See, here's the way we fill the mold." Temple closes out everything but the sand sifting through her fingers.

There it is again. What I've been watching, dreading, what even to my untutored eye looks odd. Finally, I blurt it out.

"Why isn't Temple doing what Ceelie's doing?"

"I don't know, but I think she should be." Veevee sees that her words have knocked the wind from me, but she doesn't stop. She's been a pediatric nurse during the war. "Of course, Ceelie's a few months older than Temple, and two-year-olds don't necessarily play together. But they like to play alongside of each other; they check each other out and imitate each other."

That's true. I've seen other babies do just that. But right now I want to hold back. Anything not to take that first icy plunge into what I'm not yet ready to face. I watch Ceelie: she hops up and down, gabbles, slaps at her mud pie cakes. I watch Temple: she

14

doesn't even look at us. Instead, she fixes on the sand and her fingers, her head drooping like a dahlia on a stalk.

Veevee, increasingly aware of my uneasiness, plunges on anyway.

"I know Temple can be taught to talk. I feel sure of it. I remember reading how in England during the Blitz, there were children who became speechless, but they found they could teach them to speak."

I still can't answer, but for the moment the problem moves back, not quite so suffocatingly close.

"There's a clinic at Children's Hospital. The Judge Baker Guidance Clinic. You could take Temple there. After all, how could it hurt?"

I finally find my mouth. "I'll ask my pediatrician."

My pediatrician looks Temple over: "You can take Temple to Children's Hospital if you want to, but I think you're being an anxious mother."

Perhaps, but I make an appointment anyway, with Dr. Bronson Caruthers, head of the Judge Baker Guidance Clinic.

Dr. Caruthers is avuncular and unflappable. His shaggy white hair hangs over his forehead like Will Rogers', his white doctor's coat buttons tight across his belly. He examines Temple in a friendly way, making no particular comment, and introduces Dr. Meyer, a chic European woman. Dr. Meyer brings Temple and me into her book-lined office and spreads out some toys. I'm too nervous to notice how she plays with Temple, but I'm conscious of her gentleness. Together we watch Temple.

"Well, she is certainly a very odd little girl." That's all she says. Like Veevee, Dr. Meyer confirms my anxieties; like Veevee, she makes me feel Temple's problems are solvable. From a cupboard she produces some colored plastic kitchen cups and holds them out.

"I think if you play with her with the bright colored cups … like so, see?"

Kitchen measuring cups: she's showing me how to play "give and take" with colored plastic measuring cups! Surely no one could construe measuring cups as "feckless indulgence."

I buy a set so Temple and I can play tea games at home. Temple still won't look at me, her head is still in the dahlia position, but she catches onto the game.

Though winter passes and the game improves, Temple is still aloof and mute.

March 1950. Temple is two-and-a-half. She and I rake last fall's leaves out from under the yew bushes. Our twangy metal rake is useless, so together we kneel and claw out the soggy leaf clumps with our hands. Temple is snug in her blue corduroy jacket, but her starfish fingers are turning pink with cold. I take them in my hands and blow on them. She doesn't laugh at the tickle, as would most toddlers, but she doesn't draw back. We dump the wet leaves on the compost, put away the metal rake, go in and have tea together in the plastic cups.

But she still doesn't talk; she doesn't even laugh. A few months later, when laughter finally arrives, it erupts out of her in uncontrollable spasms, along with spitting. First she spits and then she goes into a paroxysm of giggling. Both trigger her father's furious disgust.

"She's retarded! You know it, but you won't admit it!"

"She's not retarded."

"Yes, she is. You just can't face it."

"OK, for the sake of argument, let's say you're right. We'll call her 'retarded,' and I'll say I'm facing it. Now what? You want to put her in the Salvation Army box behind the A&P?"

Dick chews on the inside of his cheek. He wants to institution-alize her, has been building up to it, but knows I won't let him near the subject.

"She's the same little girl she was before you got me to call her retarded. We're not going to do anything different from what we're doing right now!"

Dick doesn't answer.

Why is he so against Temple? Her oddity isn't a personal threat to him, nor a personal dishonor. Could it be something as simple as the gap between Dick's recollection of his own childhood and what family life is like today (any family with two growing children)?

I think of Dick's upbringing. As long as he can remember, his mother has run the family establishment like clockwork—rooms swept, beds made, clothes laundered and folded. If, by some fluke, a hurricane should suddenly whirl out of nowhere, snapping tree branches in the garden and smashing the swimming pier, the next day the garden is raked clean of broken branches and, in a week, the pier rebuilt. Domestic tranquility is so immediately reestablished that one could almost believe a storm never happened. And therefore, never would.

Temple is causing storms for which there's no quick tidy-up and no immediate answer. It's a new experience for both of us, but somehow I'm able to weather it. Dick, with his strict rules of procedure, has to pack his emotional baggage very carefully before he can accept the least shift in the wind.

I think of Dick's Army report, his conviction that he knew best how to fight the war. Right after the war, he'd gone to work for the World Federalists, a group of veterans who believed in

Wendell Willkie's *One World*. Soon, convinced that the Communists were taking it over, he'd fought with the director of the World Federalists and been asked to leave. Next, he'd gone to work for his father, helping with family investments, but he and his father fought. Why, no one's told me, but for the time being neither father nor son has repaired the break. Dick's mother stops Dick from arguing further, motioning to him surreptitiously, as if soothing a restive horse.

"Shh. Don't get your father started." Later, in her abrupt fashion, she's summed up the two of them: "Dick and Jay. They both have to be right."

Dick sees his mother as perfect but has never noticed on what her perfection has to ride.

May 1950. Mrs. Grandin is dead. We've all been witness to her slow decline, seen the oxygen tent over her bed, the big red oxygen tank outside the bedroom door. But even under the oxygen tent, she's looked so much herself that her death comes as a surprise. I treasure the pretty things she's given me and recall her amused reaction when I'd said to her, "I'm trying to do my best."

"What do you think we're all trying to do?"

Even in her casket, Dick's mother looks her usual com posed and beautiful self, the breeze from an open window playing ever so slightly with the gray ostrich plumes on her long gown.

I return to Dr. Meyer for help with Temple. This time her manner is formal and brisk.

"We think you are doing a very good job, but will you please explain Mr. Grandin to me?"

What did Dick say to her? Why hasn't either of them told me? Doesn't Dr. Meyer notice my alarm? Couldn't she explain herself? Why am I unable to ask? Am I unwittingly taking on the role of non-confrontational peacemaker, as Mrs. Grandin took it on for her generation? Am I evading Dick's accusations about Temple? Not looking clearly at the issues? Turning them into jokes? Practicing being vague, even to myself? It will be years before I allow myself to conceive of such questions, years before it occurs to me that Dr. Meyer has decided she's past the point of explaining Temple to me or discussing Dick, that this is her way of telling me she's dropping Temple's case.

Whatever her reasons, I never see Dr. Meyer again. Nor will Dr. Caruthers ever make any further reference to her. A door simply closes.

I practice Bach on the piano. Temple, on the floor beside me, is absorbed in crumpling a newspaper. She squeezes it, watches it slowly spring open, shreds it, gazes at the pieces floating about her. I stop playing and try to entice her with the colored plastic cups. She stares at them for a moment, then returns to her newspaper. Again, I tell myself that children have to find their own playthings, that I mustn't always be the one to instigate the game. Yet she looks so forlorn, sitting there absorbed in her tattered plaything, sooty with newspaper ink, like a slum child nobody cares for. My pretty baby with her blue eyes and blonde curls, she who would prefer that I leave her alone. The calm, eerie snub cuts deep.

And so for today we each neglect the other. Isolated, numb, we play it safe: I in my world; she in hers. But what is her world? I turn back to the Bach. I'm not very good at it, but it's better than nothing. She hums.

She's humming the Bach.

The joy is short-lived. Tantrums are about to begin and Dick will see them as the irrefutable proof he's been looking for.

Temple rips off her lilac flowered wallpaper in long jagged shreds, digs through her blue plastic crib mattress with its bunny rabbits, claws between the springs, pulls out the stuffing, flings it about, eats it, chews it, spits it in great gray wads. She goes into a spasm of giggling and spitting. I try to calm her; she scratches free and runs out the front door. In the middle of the road, our country road with the stone wall running along it, she yanks off her clothes, squats and poops. Again, I try to scoop her up. She laughs her crazy laugh and squirms from my arms.

Back in her own room, she tears up everything, throws everything—toys, clothes, pillows, wastepaper basket. But she throws them all in the same corner of the room. Is that some kind of organization, some intention, some target she has in mind? Am I the target? I toss her a ball. She lets it bounce past her, poops again and smears her feces on the torn wallpaper.

I repaper her room and fight despair.

The tantrums don't abate. Finally in a burst of my own rage, I pick up Temple, mid-scream, carry her flailing into her room, sit her down and close the door. Let her demolish the room if she likes; she'll have to do it alone. Almost as soon as I shut the door, she stops screaming. Is it no sport to have a tantrum without an audience? Or does she really prefer to be alone?

Only in my dreams are we together. In a nightmare that repeats itself night after night, Temple comes to me, my child whom I must hold at arms' length, even to put her down in her crib. I dream that I cradle her and press her against my heart, but she turns into a rag doll. Her limp, cotton head lolls on my shoulder, no baby strength in her cloth arms and legs. Yet, I can feel her heart beat, there beating against my heart.

Sometimes in the dream she's trapped under an old wooden float, washing about in the undulating seaweed. I grope under the float, grab her bloated cotton body, and drag her up onto the float. Water streams off her, but in the center of that heap of soggy cotton, I can see her heart beating. I gather her close; I fight to keep that heartbeat going. Fight till I wake, thrashing.

My mother reacts to Temple's behavior as she might to a fart. Pay no attention and wait for the unpleasant smell to go away. It doesn't, of course, but the idea that her oldest grandchild is suffering from some sort of distasteful malfunction alarms her, especially since she's always insisted she couldn't possibly love her daughters if they weren't pretty. And, I might add, obedient.

Temple's behavior is neither obedient nor pretty, and polite pretense is probably the only response my mother can muster. Later, she'll trumpet Temple's successes, largely, I suspect, to make up for her early horror. Along with most of the women of her generation, she's grown up under Victorian constraints and has never encountered any kind of chaotic behavior nor permitted herself even the smallest emotional variety. Her concept of adventure is culled from books. Not heavy tomes. My mother prefers to entertain her mind rather than exercise it. She can't bear to read Melville: it's too dark, too difficult, too close to the Puritan bone. She prefers the chatty distance of Dickens or, perhaps, Kipling. Most of all, she loves Anthony Powell, who to me is like foregoing an African safari to take an overnight trip to "Treetops," where from the genteel comfort of a wicker armchair in an elaborate treehouse inn, you can peer down at the predictable array of animals that turn up at the water hole below.

After my sister and I, her only children, reached our late teens, our mother was torn between a fierce determination to return us to prepubertal innocence and an equally fierce determination to invade our rapidly maturing and much more interesting lives. Trapping us with amused sneers and sentimental treacle, she allowed us no rebuttal, no confrontation. There was no way to get free of her and try out life on our own. When young men began appearing, she either wanted them for herself or wanted to descant on her own girlhood triumphs which she saw as far superior. Perhaps they were; she must have been extraordinarily pretty.

Thus far, I think my mother's life depresses her. She's smart and talented but hopelessly provincial, under-educated, and untried. It all adds up to enormous ego but not the foggiest notion how to organize her intelligence to make it work for her. She has literary talent but never writes, perhaps dreading the thought that she might write something stupid and have to account for it. Or, worse yet, she might unconsciously reveal herself.

"I know exactly what I'm like," she keeps saying over and over, before either of her daughters can say it. But she doesn't know. Uninvolved, she spends her days endlessly critiquing other people and actively disapproving of me, the daughter who lunges at life from all sides. Now that I'm the mother of "a very odd little girl," it doesn't make for good social boasting.

In great distress over my mother's disapproval, I go to my Great Aunt Ruby, whose ninety-nine years have yet to dull her sharp wits. Aunt Ruby hears me out and remarks, "Well, I always thought Mary was a fool. Thrown away her talents."

Taking in Aunt Ruby's swift truth, I realize with a start that I've seen Temple's withdrawal in terms of my own need to escape my mother. I've vowed not to invade my child's life as my mother tries to invade mine. If Temple doesn't want me, I'll keep my distance. I will not be like my mother. But Temple is only a baby.

Then comes an appalling thought: so am I! Guilt takes hold of me.

"Rubbish!" says Aunt Ruby. "Guilt is useless and irrelevant. If you really think you're guilty through a neglect you haven't even understood, then figure out how to help Temple now, and use your guilt to fire yourself up to do it."

In the moment of her words, I understand my own odd prayer: "Give me back my child." It isn't just about Temple; it's about both of us. We've each gone away from the other to somewhere quite far off.

"Thrown away her talents." Now the second part of Aunt Ruby's words sounds its note.

"Are you telling me my mother hasn't lived up to her potential, and the loss of it has been her folly?"

"Your mother's life is your mother's life. If Temple is to survive, then so must you. But as yourself, not as your mother's idea of who she'd like you to be."

With those releasing words, I allow myself to see my mother in a new light—appealingly pretty but choosing to persist in deliberate innocence, trapped forever between two gold mirrors. They're beautiful mirrors but positioned in such a way that each reflects her in the other, creating an endless hall of repeated images. Nothing will ever change in those images: nothing added and nothing taken away, just each reflection growing a little smaller than the one in front of it, until at last nothing is discernible.

Chapter 2

As the Twig Is Bent

If I'm going to guide Temple, if I'm going to stand up for her in any positive way, I must have help. But who? And what kind of help?

By some miracle I find and hire a nanny who's cared for "a little boy with problems like Temple's." Where I learn of her and how we get in touch, I have no recollection. Even when we meet, we're neither of us quite sure what we're talking about.

"I think I know how to help." That's all the nanny says. "I had good results with the little boy."

She shows me the learning cards she used with him, the games and coloring books she plans to use to hold Temple's attention. "What's important is to keep Temple involved and not to let her slip off into daydreaming."

"Involved." Yes. Together, we'll pull Temple into our world. Every so often there are signs that she wants to be in it—like her humming the Bach.

The nanny comes to live with us, and her games have the same feel as Dr. Meyer's game with the plastic cups. The nanny is better than I am at holding Temple's attention, so I turn my attention to making home life smooth, hoping Dick will forget his uneasiness over his child.

*

Six months pass. Temple has responded to the nanny's teachings, but she still doesn't talk. Now that she's three, Dr. Caruthers recommends that she come to the Children's Hospital for a ten-day observational visit, also to have an electroencephalogram (EEG).

"An EEG will settle the question of her singular moments of stillness, her apparent tuning out. It could be an indication of petit mal." (a form of mild epilepsy)

I agree to both the EEG and the ten-day hospital visit.

Temple doesn't seem to mind the visit. Like the life jacket episode on South Beach, neither sad nor mad, she's strangely indifferent to her new surroundings. Nor does she seem to mind when I leave her in the company of a friendly nurse. Oblivious to my goodbyes, she's entirely absorbed with picking out a red crib to sleep in. It's I who feels the wrench.

The EEG is another story. Temple rages at the violation of her space. Her face turns scarlet; her hair is soaked from flinging her head about. Finally the anesthesia takes over; her screams turn to hiccuping sobs, and she falls asleep.

To everyone's relief, the EEG shows no brain damage, no retardation, and no sign of petit mal.

The next day when I come to the hospital, I'm not allowed to visit with Temple but must watch her through a one-way mirror. The room is full of children, but Temple sits by herself on the floor near the door. Dr. Caruthers pushes a slip of paper under the door; she pushes it back. Over and over, the two of them do this.

"See? She's responding," he observes comfortingly. "That's some kind of two-way game."

Is it? She can't see you. To me it's just as solitary as bouncing a ball against a wall and catching it on return.

Next, Dr. Caruthers wants Temple's hearing tested and recommends an ear specialist named Dr. Onesti. For the first time, he implies a character judgment, something, perhaps, in the nature of a caution. He tosses it out to me in a gruff, offhanded way.

"I want you to understand before we have our joint meeting that Dr. Onesti chooses to wear those long earrings. I don't know why—that's her affair—and, ah, a bit too much make-up. But, that's all right. She's a wonderful doctor, the best in the field, the very best." He keeps on assuring me of Dr. Onesti's excellence, almost begging me to look beyond the Christmas decorations.

After the hearing test, Dick and I assemble with Dr. Caruthers for the conference. In comes Dr. Onesti in her white medical coat and her long earrings. She's a very pretty Italian girl, and her earrings are very pretty. She sits down, crosses her legs, her legs are very pretty too. How delightfully exotic she must look to a conservative Boston medic, her earrings dancing in distracting contrast to her white medical jacket. I can't help but wonder if Dr. Caruthers' caution might not be for himself, a fear that he could be relishing Dr. Onesti's prettiness rather more than he should, considering his age, his position, his Yankee-ness.

We confer together. Though Temple still isn't talking, Dr. Onesti has found no hearing loss.

"Well, I think Temple will learn to talk," Dr. Caruthers assures us, "but let's see if we can't speed up the process. There's a wonderful speech teacher in Belmont: Mrs. Reynolds. She gets amazing results. She's very kind, I think Temple will take to her. She has a little school in her own house. Yes, I think she's just the one to help."

Mrs. Reynolds, white-haired and dear, proves to be everything Dr. Caruthers has said. Temple goes to her three times a week for both individual speech therapy and a small nursery school class. The class is in Mrs. Reynolds' basement and consists of a handful of children with mixed abilities: some retarded, some Down Syndrome, all with varying degrees of speech problems. I decide not to let Dick see the school. For the time being he's at peace with the diagnosis that Temple isn't retarded, but I fear if he sees those little Down Syndrome children, he may take up his obsession again.

At home, the nanny continues her lessons, introducing Temple to the notion that there are other people in the world and, like it or not, she must learn to take turns with them. A beachhead in Temple's isolation? I admire the nanny's effort, and, for the most part, it works. But as yet, I see no sign that Temple will ever want to share her toys, projects, time, or affection with another child. And the nanny is cruel to the sibling; her focus and love go only to Temple. The nanny is older than I. Strong-willed, ready to override me at every turn, she's trapped me in a devil's bargain. She knows that I need her to help with Temple, knows I need her presence to keep the household running smoothly, allaying Dick's anxieties. She knows too that, as Temple is gaining a foothold on life, Dick and I are losing ours.

Finally, I screw up my courage. Despite the closed door, I make a personal call to Dr. Meyer and tell her I'm having problems with my marriage. Her only comment is, "These things happen." She suggests a psychiatrist who specializes in marriage counseling, a dear wise man I will go to for years.

The next time I call Dr. Caruthers' office, I'm told that the department thinks that Temple should see a child psychiatrist. Meaning what? That Dr. Caruthers functions only as a diagnostician? That he knows we have family problems? All I have to go on is a departmental recommendation that Temple should be under the care of a young Viennese doctor whose first request is a session with Temple's parents.

Winter 1951. Temple's new doctor is reading a notebook that lies open on his desk, its pages handwritten in tight cursive, the grooves of its cramped loops almost cutting through the paper.

The doctor is slight, blonde, good-looking. An arrogant Austrian, a skier perhaps. Perhaps a Jew who has fled Europe before WWII. He has a European accent like Dr. Meyer's, only more sibilant, more like a war movie Nazi. He stands to greet us. I'm taller than he and I sense it annoys him. He returns quickly to the chair behind his power desk, to his study of the notebook.

Dick and I wait for him to speak. I wonder why we're here. What are we supposed to confide in him and how will it help Temple? Dick chews the inside of his cheek and avoids my eye. He's returned lately to his daily thrashing of words—why I'm not sure because Temple's doing quite well. No, she still can't talk, but she's begun; she's trying. Yes, she still has tantrums, but not so often and not such big ones. Improvement, isn't that the point?

Dick doesn't think so: "We've been recommended to a psychiatrist, who wants to see us first. Doesn't that ring a bell with you?"

Should it? How do I know Dick isn't right? Despite Aunt Ruby's bracing words, maybe I am guilty. I've been harboring secret thoughts of leaving my marriage, but I don't want to leave. I fear if I leave I'll no longer be a good person, fear letting go, fear losing some small kernel of hope that I might still be a good person.

I'm unnerved by the doctor, unnerved by his psychiatric expertise. He's supposed to help Temple, but already he's advising us in his sibilant accent that, when Temple reaches her teens, she should be psychoanalyzed. What does he think she'll reveal about herself when she's a teenager? Or about me? Pieces of me are already missing. Between Temple and Dick, I've pushed them down a black hole.

Will the doctor define Temple? Will he name her disorder as Adam named the animals? Dick likes names, hounds me with them, forces me into corners—sharp black and white corners that allow no escape.

"Retardation," Dick says.

"It's not that simple," I counter.

"It is simple. You make it complicated, so you won't have to look at what you've done."

"What have I done?"

Dick makes no answer, his focus is on a win-lose battle. Thus far, he sees my insistence that Temple's improved as my having won the first round, and it infuriates him. Fury has become his attack weapon, his release from tension, his aphrodisiac. It has a rhythm now, like sex. I have sex with him to contain his fury, but it doesn't assuage his burning need to be right.

"When I married you, you were a good girl."

I'm no longer good?

"When I married you, you were economical."

"Temple has serious medical problems."

Dick doesn't accept that as an answer. He has money, old, conservative money that talks to him in neat balance sheets, and it annoys him to spend it on Temple. Yet, he would pay for an institution, pay more than he pays now, if only to prove he's right. Long ago his money talked to me; it seemed like a romantic largesse out of Scott Fitzgerald. I didn't know then how it could be used to pinch life into the sharp, angled cursive that I recognize now, upside down in the notebook in front of the doctor.

Please God, what has Dick written? Did Dick send that note-book to Dr. Meyer? And has she sent it on to this doctor? Did Dr. Meyer tell this doctor about my request for a marriage coun-selor? My own handwriting is schoolgirlish and will never have the strength to hold out against those tight bands of cursive. Dick has also taken to writing me accusing letters and leaving them on my side of the bed. He lifts words out of my mouth and reshapes them to his own argument.

"Yes, that's what I said," I say, trying to defend my intention, "but that's not what I meant."

The doctor looks down at Dick's notebook. His lips are pursed. I wait for his sibilant words. My heart thuds. The veins in my hands swell up with shame. I hold still, hold very still as I've learned to do. Stare at my swollen hands and watch like a rabbit out the corner of my eye. The doctor has only to flash his badge; expertise is my enemy. I fear its flick lash and brace myself like a child called into the principal's office.

"It is autism. Infant schizophrenia."

Dick picks up the doctor's words and runs with them. Face tight, eyes stern, mind racing along the same old kenneled inten-tion, he gives himself permission to name his child "unaccept-able."

Just as quickly, comes the doctor's backtracking denial. "I did-n't say that, I said she manifested autistic symptoms."

Too late, the words have escaped. Loosed from their human code, they're already metastasizing. I sense danger but don't see how to fight it. I know the good man Dick wants to be, but I also know his impatience with any argument but his own. Most of all, I know his commitment to rules and authority: "If somebody will just tell me what to do," he says repeatedly, "I'll do it."

Now the words have told him what to do.*

*

The next time I see Temple's doctor, I'm alone. He's had a session alone with Temple. He tells me that Temple has been psychotic, an infant schizophrenic, but that now she's convalescing and has become a neurotic.

Like the rest of us?

The doctor looks at me as if he smells something faintly unpleasant, and names me an hysteric. "Oil and water don't mix," he says. "There is no teamwork between an obsessive like your husband and an hysteric."

I'm not sure what "hysteric" means and am afraid to ask. Later, I learn that in Victorian terms, it means a woman who is too much the individualist; in Freudian terms, it's a woman who wants a penis. Not knowing either definition, not even sure what he means by "obsessive," I show no reaction; I smile tentatively, hoping to please him, praying he has the solution, the key, the formula. It's like a spy scene. What does he want from me? What am I supposed to know that he's looking for?

Was I depressed when she was born? he asks. No, I answer, then try to explain that Dick doesn't have very many friends. He says that's "quite suitable," he knows many men like that. He purses his lips. How many friends do I have?

I try to think. Finally, I say, "three close friends in the winter, two where we go in the summer."

He approves of this. "One should not have too many good friends."

Does "too many" mean shallow? I don't know. Much later, I learn this is the first test, and I've passed it.

---

* "Language is as vital to the physician's art as the stethoscope or the scalpel...Of all the words the doctor uses, the name he gives the illness has the greatest weight. It forms the foundation of all subsequent discussion, not only between doctor and patient but also between doctor and doctor and between patient and patient. The name of the illness becomes part of the identity of the sufferer." Jerome Groopman, M.D. *The New Yorker* 11/13/2003

I try to convince myself that I like this doctor, but we don't smile; we don't joke. I have no medical experience with psychiatrists, so I don't know if jokes are allowed. I think of an old boyfriend, also a psychiatrist, who used to love jokes. I know the doctor knows this man and doesn't like him, hasn't liked him since the two men interned together. Now he questions me about him, presses me on our relationship. Out of curiosity? Dislike? Why can't I in return ask him why he hates my old boyfriend?

The doctor suggests that perhaps Temple should be in a foster home. My stunned face betrays me and he drops the subject as fast as he's brought it up. Next, he instructs me to tell my husband to stop using the word "schizophrenic." I don't dare say that he's the one who used it first. Another thought. Have he and Dick been talking together alone? About what?

Suddenly, curiously, I hear the doctor exclaim that he wished he hadn't used the word "schizophrenic." It's our first spark of friendship.

I go home. I continue to drive Temple to Mrs. Reynolds three times a week. I hide my feelings, to protect Temple, to keep us both safe. Or is it to keep me frozen so I won't feel the despair that descends after each of Dick's tirades?

"She's insane." He now has psychiatric proof. "You won't admit it; that's why you won't institutionalize her!"

How do I know he isn't right?

One night comes the big weep: such hard sobbing, I think I'm going to strangle on my own tears. Great salt gobbets of grief are stuck in my throat. The next morning I wake exhausted and promise myself that never again as long as I live will I cry that hard. Then comes an odd sense of relief. I've peered into the black hole, and I'm still alive. I've named my despair and this sunny morning I'm living with it and it's almost a friend. I make my first big resolve: whatever the stakes, whatever the odds, I will not let Dick put Temple in an institution. I'll take it one day at a time, as the alcoholics do.

I make a second resolve: I will keep my head up out of the dark; I'll allow myself to breathe. Have I been holding my breath all this time? Yes, and it's been keeping me from thinking. I'll breathe; I'll think.

First thought: between the nanny and Mrs. Reynolds, Temple has improved markedly. I can see that for myself, so forget Dick's argument that I'm in denial.

Second thought: the reason I can never win an argument with Dick is because he's too impatient to hear me out and get my point. Instead, he latches onto the first peripheral that will justify what he wants to justify and shouts me down. So, forget trying to show him how Temple—a living, growing child—is improving. He's made up his mind she's a capital investment: she should be institutionalized because that's what the medical authorities are prescribing these days, and he's put a lot of money into their advice. Unfortunately, that's a point in his favor. We live in a conservative world where those deemed "unfit" are routinely separated out and institutionalized.

"Unfit for what?" I ask, unwilling to give in.

For a moment Dick looks baffled, then bullies his way back to where he started. "It's not the way it's supposed to go!"

The specter of Bruno Bettelheim rears its head. His book, *The Empty Fortess*, is on the bestseller list and everybody thinks he's a genius. Bettelheim believes that autistic children behave like concentration camp inmates, that they suffer from the same helplessness as prisoners who've given up hope, that they are wasting away like prisoners who refuse to eat, that they avert their gaze, as did prisoners who avoided eye contact with the guards. Bettelheim believes autistic children, like concentration camp inmates, are trying to blot out an immediate, threatening reality—the SS in the camps, their mothers in the home.*

Does the Viennese doctor believe in Bettelheim? Why not? Both men are European; both look to be Freudian. Is it possible that the doctor feels guilty to have escaped the Nazis, while Bettelheim was forced to suffer Dachau? Not impossible. Nevertheless, even if that's so and I'm really the horrible creature Bettelheim's diagnosis says I am, then why try to please one of his disciples?

Holding on tight to these first shaky steps to maturity, I pick up another thought. What could have caused the rift between Temple's doctor, an arrogant, proper European, and my old boyfriend, a lanky, laconic Westerner from Nebraska? The boyfriend was brilliant, irreverent, and funny—one of Oppenheimer's fair-haired boys before he switched from physics to psychiatry. Had he made fun of the Viennese doctor when the two of them were interning? The doctor was an easy mark; Germans don't get our tongue-in-cheek irony. They don't understand Jimmy Stewart.

A chink, I think I found a chink! The doctor is human. He will no longer intimidate me.

Ah, but with a heavy heart, I guess I'll have to accept his diagnosis. Temple may well be suffering from infant schizophrenia, brought on by a psychosocial trauma. And maybe, just maybe— even if I didn't mean to—I'm the one who brought it on.

Boy, that's a bitter pill.

OK, I accept it, but, as Aunt Ruby advised, I won't weep and wail. If Temple's problem is psychosocial, then it's time to look for psychosocial clues.

---

* Richard Pollack. *The Creation of Dr. B: A Biography of Bruno Bettelheim*, Simon & Schuster, NY, 1997.

First, I thumb through old college textbooks, get as far as the startled response and feel waves of boredom creeping over me. The plodding, literal focus of Psych. 101 offers no clues to autism, so as fast as I can I turn back to my true love, which is literature. At least literature will give me the illusion of addressing Temple's problems while allowing me to run away from them. But something's changed. Now I find I'm drawn like a magnet to Victorian novels full of dark family secrets and wicked, autocratic men. I'm also drawn to Victorian ghost stories, perhaps because what lurks about, unspoken, between Dick and me feels sort of like a ghost. Most of the time we talk practicalities but always hovering around the edge are the unanswered questions about Temple: like why had Dr. Meyer come up with her demand that I explain Dick to her. What did he say to her unbeknownst to me? And what has he written to the new doctor? Where did the new doctor get the idea of farming Temple out to a foster family? I like to think Dick cares for Temple, but I wouldn't want to bet on it. For the time being, he simply allows her to exist under the same roof.

Continuing my literary search, I prowl around in the spoiled, uneasy world of Scott Fitzgerald, then, best yet, I light on Henry James. Here are social battles I know by heart: women struggling to hold their own in a Boston only two generations removed from the one I live in. James' understanding of the way in which we are both the product and victim of the society we live in leads me to read Erik Erikson's recently published *Childhood and Society*. An innovative leader in the field of psychoanalysis and human development, Erikson writes that our psyche is made up of more than a Freudian ego developing in lonely isolation. Coining the term "identity," Erikson describes us as a combination of individual development, family, community, and nation. All these elements impact on our ego, and our ego on them.

Well, if that's so, then what's going on between Dick, Temple's new doctor, and me?

First, there's the young Viennese doctor, disciplined in old-world Freud, seeing his future in the United States as a psychiatrist in the growing field of disturbed children. But, still a European, perhaps not fully acclimated to our culture, our particular subtleties?

Then there's Dick, WWII vet, reared in patrician Boston, seeing his future as a paterfamilias, carving the Sunday roast as his father has before him, his children watching, their faces washed, their hands in their laps. Afterwards a Sunday walk perhaps, with the youngest child riding on his shoulders.

Last comes me. More than twelve years younger than either man, the first college female in my family, in my neighborhood, freshly hatched from postwar Harvard, from classes filled with vets on the G.I. Bill of Rights. Not college kids, but men in their late twenties who've left pieces of themselves behind on various battlefronts: Men who've faced the worst, who are afraid of nothing, and aren't about to swallow Harvard whole. I've watched these men stand up in the middle of government lectures, challenge the professor, question his theories, even his facts. Their words are still in my ears. I've seen their crutches, their empty sleeves; I've caught their fever, their fervor, an under ripple of "beat" rebellion that won't fully surface for another fifteen years. They're my idea of the future.

What none of the three of us has yet noticed is that the fifties are already detaching into two separate futures: the bebop, beat world, and the suburban "Leave-it-to-Beaver" world. Each sees the other as worthless, neither speaking to the other. I see the "beat" world as exciting, immoral, and grungy. I see the "Leave-it-to-Beaver" world as serene, obedient and temptingly pretty, yet, somehow, never quite real. Part of me keeps thinking I can make it real simply by being obedient to it. The other part keeps breaking loose and running for dear life to the creative life of Harvard and Cambridge.

Two separate cultures. Can I live with a foot in each? Am I

striking out on my own or am I, like Temple, a schizophrenic?

I begin a long slide into theory. I figure if I can tie the scary facts of autism in with what I'm reading, find in Henry James, Erik Erikson, and English eccentricity some kind of all-encompassing life vision, I'll get a handle on the reality of our lives and be able to accept it. But reality keeps escaping behind the scenery, waiting to pop out and scare me again. I'm alone in the prim fifties with a child who doesn't want me and a husband who isn't sure he wants his child.

Ultimately, a hunger for meaning will lead me to a deeper study of autism but not until it has journeyed through my consciousness for many years. For now, it joins forces with myth.

The dictionary defines myth as a person or thing existing only in imagination, but when I come upon the old changeling myth, I know it's no thing of imagination. A changeling must have been a child with autism.

According to Celtic mythology, changelings are fairy children. Endowed with mysterious powers—both generous and spiteful, friendly and malevolent—the one thing fairies lack is the capacity for human feeling. And, because of the lack, they want to join us, inspire us, but then will extract a cruel and capricious price.

Before a mortal baby is christened, the Celtic warning goes, don't let her wear green ribbons, for the fairies will see the green and steal her away to replenish their empty hearts. They'll put one of their own in her place; it will look like your child, but it will be sickly and odd and will want to be left alone. Remembering its forest home, it will cling to a block of wood, giving its loyalty only to the wood. Instead of speaking, it will hum and make strange croaking noises. And, if you are so unwise as to try to caress it, it will laugh and spit and take revenge on you with obscene tricks. A changeling baby has no Christian soul. It must be thrown on the fire. The purifying flames will strip it of its enchanted shape, so it will have no choice but to fly back to its fairy home.

Changelings, I learn, were part of the ancient Celtic earth rites which didn't start to give way to Christianity until after 500 A.D. Green, the color of nature, was the fairy color. Fairies, like nature, were thought to be beautiful, bounteous with gifts, but capricious. Like nature, they could snatch away their bounty at a moment's notice, blight your crops, sicken the livestock, and level your barn with a single storm.

The country folk of the Middle Ages understood physical deformity. Their countryside abounded in cripples and idiots. But a spiritual monster—hiding in the body of a beautiful child—that was demonic.

Temple is a beautiful child, but her beauty is uncanny. She still doesn't speak, still won't look at me, and if she does, she appears to look beyond me into some private land of enchantment. She no longer plays with her feces, but she still has tantrums, still goes into wild giggling and spitting. Though I must clean up after her, I'm not allowed to join her in that enchanted land.

Tantrums are hard to handle, and fecal smears are smelly, but exclusion breaks the heart.

I ride horseback early in the morning before anyone is up. The groom from the local stable has to exercise the horses then, and he knows all the bridle paths. Together we ride through the leafy woods and across an open meadow, later to become a mall.

In the meadow, a mother pheasant flutters in front of us trailing her wing in the long grass to fool us into thinking she's wounded, enticing us to catch her, leading us further and further from her nest in the clover where her young are hidden. I feel a sudden love for her this soft green morning. She keeps on with her trick, dragging her wing, improvising a wound, risking her safety for the safety of her young.

To Hell with Bettelheim—and diagnosis—and myths! I, too, will improvise for the safety of my young.

✳

June 1952. Miracle of miracles. Temple's been with Mrs. Reynolds a little over two years, and she's learned to speak! Not just single words, whole sentences are tumbling out! She's also learned the rudiments of kindergarten: a little group discipline, a little waiting your turn to recite, your turn for a glass of juice.

Though Temple is not yet five, Mrs. Reynolds and the social worker from the Belmont School System both feel she's ready for a month at St. Hubert's, a camp for special children run by Mrs. Huckle, an English woman.

It's a blazing hot afternoon. Dick, Temple, and I rattle down a dirt road through the pine woods and out onto a stubbled clearing. Long trestle tables are set under a solitary apple tree and behind them lie a cluster of low wooden buildings. From one of the buildings, her arms held wide to greet us, emerges Mrs. Huckle, the epitome of matriarchy in a vast pair of flowing, black velvet pajamas. Tilted on her gray shingled bob is a floppy black velvet tam, which gives her the look of the old British actress, Margaret Rutherford. I trust her from the start. Not only does she resemble Margaret Rutherford, she gives out the same aura of authority, good sense, and theatrical timing. She claps her hands, and a flock of children come running out. One by one, she makes them introduce themselves—easier for some than others. Next, she looks at Temple.

"Temple, you may come to my camp, but by the end of the summer you must have learned two things. You must learn to say the *Lord's Prayer* and you must learn—always—to do your veddy, veddy best." That's a tall order for a little autistic girl who's only just accomplished the nearly impossible feat of human speech.

Mrs. Huckle soon charms Dick with a description of her long-gone school on the Riviera for the sons of maharajahs. He, in turn, charms her with his story of World War II tank service in the Battle of the Bulge and his French girlfriend in Nancy.

Behind Mrs. Huckle, pacing amiably under the apple tree, is her small, white-haired, and totally silent husband. After introducing him, she gives him no further reference, so what role he fulfills, I haven't a clue. Mrs. Huckle doesn't say why or how her Riviera school ended, nor why she's come to this country and not to England. But I feel certain that whatever her fortunes and whomever her enemies, she's met both in her black velvet pajamas and tam, undaunted and unimpressed.

What a splendid influence for anybody.

By the end of the summer, Temple's learned to say the *Lord's Prayer* and to do her "veddy, veddy best," something she'll pretty much stick to from now on. In September, Mrs. Huckle feels that she's capable of entering regular kindergarten in a small school, if the school understands her history.

I arrange to meet with Mr. Everett Ladd, headmaster of the Dedham Country Day School, and Mrs. Dietsch, the head of the first three grades. I tell them Temple's story, and Mr. Ladd's response is positive.

"Yes, of course we'll take her. We're educators; that's what we think we should be doing."

He has two requests: "First, let us stay in close communication. If there's any kind of difficulty, we want to be able to talk it over with you honestly. If that's not possible, then teaching will be impossible too."

The second request comes from Mrs. Dietsch.

"If Temple has a bad day, may we send her home?"

"Yes, of course."

Of course, Temple does have bad days, and Mrs. Dietsch does send her home—days of mortifying tantrums, the worst being the day she bit Mrs. Dietsch. Mrs. Dietsch uses the bad days to explain to the rest of the class that Temple has problems, and they will have to be understanding. With her intuitive sense of what a child like Temple needs, Mrs. Dietsch also teaches me.

"I always put my hand on Temple's shoulder when I lean over to help her," she tells me. "It makes her jump, but I keep it there anyway. Gently, but firmly." Very plucky of Mrs. Dietsch, considering that Temple may well throw another fit and bite her again.

On the whole—give or take the fussing for extra attention, even the tantrums—Temple does amazingly well at Dedham Country Day, and manages to keep up with the rest of the class.

Temple and I visit her doctor together now. First, he talks to her alone and then to me alone. He's delighted and puzzled by Temple's progress.

"I do not understand why she got ill," he says in his Viennese accent. "And I do not understand why she is getting well."

Is he beginning to question the gospel of Bettelheim?

November 1953. A third sibling is born. I carry him home in my arms, and, sitting in the kitchen, unfold his blankets to show the two other children their new baby brother.

As the baby grows, Temple is not much interested, but her sister, enchanted to have a live, live-in doll, considers the baby her property, and takes over his introduction to life and friends. I see her now lugging him about, hardly bigger herself, talking to him, instructing him. He grins over her shoulder, his bare toes, scraping along the rug, the floor, the grass, the dirt, the gravel. He doesn't mind his toes; he adores her company.

Chapter 3

Childhood

In the years between 1954 and 1958, years when Temple was very much part of school and community life, what helps most is the "Leave-it-to-Beaver Moms' Union." The "Union" is an agreed-upon code of behavior all neighborhood moms expect from every child. The warning, "I'm going to tell your mother," goes for anyone about to veer into unacceptable behavior, and Temple is no exception.

Yes, Temple still has tantrums and, no, they're never easy. The tricky part is figuring out what she really can't manage and when she's using a tantrum to get her own way. There's a bit of the manipulator in all of us.

Fifty years into the future, I'll run into a "union mom" from those days—both of us old ladies now—and thank her from the bottom of my heart for always making sure Temple was included. She recalls how her own child wanted to exclude Temple from his birthday party. "You know the rule," I told him. "Everybody comes; otherwise, no party."

Mrs. Dietsch at Dedham Country Day says some children can read by first grade; some can't. By third grade, she says, learning to read is crucial. Could I help teach Temple?

"I'll do what I can."

Back in my own childhood, when I was still too young to go to school, I'd picked up reading without knowing what I was doing.

Reading, I'd been told, was something I'd learn in first grade. When I got to first grade we were each handed a copy of *Dick and Jane* which I could read at a glance, but that didn't seem to be what reading was. Reading seemed to be taking a long time looking at each page, then reciting the words in a funny, halting voice. I couldn't figure out why, but I'd been raised not to ask a lot of silly questions, so I fidgeted around until it was my turn, then put on the same halting voice. It was terribly hard work and boring beyond belief, but nobody said reading would be easy.

It doesn't take much to figure that Temple might be going through the same boredom, and it's blowing her circuits. I look through the bookcase, pull out *The Wizard of Oz,* and show it to her. She likes the pictures, so I read her a bit of it to get us into the story and then stop. "Tell you what: I'll read the next paragraph, then you can read the one after it." I cheat a bit at first, reading more than a paragraph to get us further into the story. By the time it's Temple's turn, she wants to know what happens next and is eager to sound out the words phonetically, each syllable worth the effort. Next she's racing along way past her paragraph, caught in the grip of a good yarn.

Clothes are a problem for Temple. There are some she'll wear and some she won't, yet curiously, there are clothes she complains about endlessly and wears anyway. She fusses over her scratchy Sunday petticoat but she always puts it on, in fact, she seems to want to wear it. When I ask her why, she says it's because she knows it's expected of her, just as she knows she's expected to sit through Sunday dinner without squirming or complaining. Other people's expectations have entered her reality.

"Besides, Sunday dinner is quiet. It's noise and confusion I hate."

With projects, Temple's learned that, if she wants the other children to help her with her project, she'll have to show some kind of interest in theirs. With games, she's learned that if she doesn't want to be left out, she'll have to be a good sport whether she feels like it or not. But, when it comes to table manners, she won't close her mouth and doesn't give a hoot if her eating style, or lack of it, disturbs her mother's prissy idea of Miss Manners. That is, until one lunch hour at Dedham Country Day School when she eats opposite another classmate. "Urp! Blaaah! Yuck! Charlie doesn't close his mouth, and the food goes round and round. It looks like a garbage truck!" Then a thought. "Is that how I look?"

For the first time Temple's really looked at another child, seen how he eats and figured out that, if she looks like Charlie, nobody will want to eat with her. From now on she closes her mouth when she eats.

Sportsmanship, however, continues to be a problem. Though Temple's learned to shape up in the give and take of the schoolroom, she still doesn't quite grasp the notion of schoolyard games. It's due partly to a lack of gaming instinct and partly to the praise she's learned to expect for mastering the daily snags of life. Not surprisingly, she interprets a game as one more activity deserving of the usual praise. When she loses and praise is not forthcoming, she gets furious and doesn't mind telling everybody. The siblings, mortified by her behavior in front of their friends— who are happy to point it out—break the family rule of limiting outrage to low mutters of "not fair" and yell along with the other kids: "Bad sport! Sore loser!" Temple goes into a major blow-up. The game is OVER!

Nevertheless, she likes to play double solitaire with her father. Double solitaire demands attention, speed, and timing—traits that run strong in the Grandin family, and the point isn't sportsmanship; the point is to win. They both enjoy the game, and Dick, in spite of himself, finds he has a grudging affection for Temple.

Temple makes up for her lack of sportsmanship with projects. Her bedroom is boobytrapped with them. Anybody opening the door is instantly entangled, garroted or sliced across the face by a series of strings cross-hatching her room. The top red string lowers the shade; the lower red one raises it. The yellow string turns on the light, and the white string runs out a sign that reads: "ENTER AT YOUR OWN RISK!"

In the middle of it all stands her wooden bed, either red or a bilious shade of salmon, depending on which side of the bed you're looking at. That's because, as a family project, we'd elected one Sunday to paint the bed red and had run low on paint. The Vineyard Haven hardware store wasn't open, so we'd added white to what was left of the red, thinking it wouldn't show. It doesn't show to Temple; it only shows to her mother, whose delicate color sense is deeply offended but not offended enough to repaint the bed.

On the salmon side of the bed, in a metal cage, lives Crusader Mouse, a present to Temple from her buddy, Lyman, who lives next door to us in Dedham. Crusader's white back is often painted with a red cross of Mercurochrome to make him look like a Red Cross knight. Each morning, as one of her projects, Temple makes Crusader run along her room strings.

One morning the children come to me in great distress.

"Crusader's lying on the floor of his cage, He looks dead." We decide to take him to the vet.

"Is he really dead?" The vet nods. "Was it because we painted him with Mercurochrome?"

"No. The Mercurochrome wouldn't hurt him."

"We wanted him to look like a Crusader Knight."

"How long have you had Crusader?"

"A couple of years. He belonged to Lyman first."

"How long did Lyman have him?" Everybody looks at each other. Nobody can remember.

"A couple of years, maybe. A long time anyway."

"That's a very old mouse. Crusader's lived a long and happy life. He died in his sleep."

"Oh." Relief. Then a new idea.

"Can we have a funeral?"

I think we do, though, in truth, I don't remember. I'm sure it was a grand funeral with a tin cookie box for a coffin and hymns and "Amens" and a long, talky obit. We're a family of talkers and, by now, Temple is no exception.

Talk isn't the only family trait we all share. Temple and I both have a tendency to enjoy a somewhat rebellious streak; you might call it a renegade gene. But, to balance it off, we also share a caution gene. If you look at the family tree, you can see that both traits have been around for generations. The renegade gene isn't a big one. As a family, we're basically law-abiding. But, if given a chance, we tend to like to go a deviant route. Temple enjoys boasting to me of her minor infractions of the law.

"Where it says, 'Keep within the line'," she announces with great glee, "I like to walk just outside it."

However, there's a point at which caution takes over. Temple doesn't like it when Mrs. Dietsch sends her home from school for unacceptable behavior, nor does she like it when her mother and Mrs. Dietsch compare notes. Her caution gene cautions her to shape up, and it talks louder than her autism.

Old Mr. Grandin worries when I allow Temple to pedal her bike down a three-mile stretch of road to the Vineyard Haven Pottery shed where the children make pots out of Gay Head clay.

"She's a good bike rider," I tell him. "She watches out for cars. The road's straight, and anybody coming can see her." I also know, though autism may flare up under fatigue or tension, I can count on Temple. I recognize her caution as my own.

Temple's birthday is August twenty-ninth, and her birthday party is always a big summer feature. In the past, old Mr. Grandin has given parties for the Vineyard children, so he enjoys being part of Temple's celebration. Katharine Noonan, his cook, always bakes and frosts a beautiful birthday cake, decorating it with blossoms from the Rose of Sharon bush in his garden.

This summer when Temple's birthday rolls round, the striped bass are running early. It looks as if a fishing expedition with Roland Otier would make a great birthday party. Roland is the local fishing expert; he always knows where the stripers are running.

August twenty-ninth dawns gray and windless, but we take off in Roland's boat anyway. Alas, we soon find the boat is rolling from one listless sea swell to the next. Fishing lines droop. Children droop. The heaving ocean is making them seasick. Roland and I look at each other. Should we give up and go home? No, says Roland, let's hold out till the tide turns. It seems Roland knows something I don't know about the nature of tide and fish.

We hold out for the tide-turn and with it, everybody's line gives a jump. We pull in fish, the like of which none of us has seen before nor will again—one after another, hand over hand, huge stripers, too feisty to reel in with a rod, too weighty for the children to haul in without Roland's help. The children squeal and hop up and down. The stripers leap to break free, their black dotted backs and silver bellies glistening in the boat's wake. We have supper of striper for days.

At the Saturday night Vineyard dances, children and grown-ups dance together and play games. Temple's favorite game is musical chairs. Musical chairs demands no sportsmanship, only those Grandin traits of attention, speed, and timing. However, she has a formidable opponent in a distinguished old gentleman whose enthusiasm for the game sometimes gets the better of his sense of fair play. At such times, a father is delegated to tap him on the back and remind him that, though we all play musical chairs, the game is really for the children.

Once when the gentleman was locked in fierce competition with a child—I like to think it was Temple—his elderly sister rushed to her brother's defense.

"You have to understand," she explained to the delegated father, "Gerald wasn't born in 'givvy' weather."

Indeed he wasn't. No believer in fair play, he had amassed a vast fortune by never giving an opponent a sporting chance.

Beyond musical chairs and double solitaire with her father, Temple's a child who never likes to join an organized sports activity if she can possibly avoid it. Summer projects outside of our home have to be devised in order to help her make a connection to other people.

Knowing that Temple likes to sew and is good at it, I visit a dressmaker in Edgartown who alters clothes. I tell her about Temple's skill with the needle, but I also tell her about her problems. If she'll take Temple on, she will work hard for her, but, if Temple proves difficult, I will, of course, pay her for having given Temple a chance.

"No pay. I'd be happy to do it," the dressmaker says. "I could use some help, and I got a kid with problems myself."

Temple goes to work for her hemming dresses and doing whatever sewing jobs she's asked to do. The dressmaker pays Temple handsomely. I demur.

"No, sir. Temple earned that money. She worked hard. She was a real help." Temple is so proud. After she's grown up, Temple will embroider herself a cowboy shirt with a steer head. I bet she still has it.

And so on and so on. The days of Temple's childhood in the comfortable, Leave-it-to-Beaver world of Dedham and the Vineyard could be the days from any privileged childhood. What was unique for her was the safe cocoon they provided. There would be other later environments, but those two habitats were Temple's greatest salvation.

Dick and I decide to take a trip alone to Europe. Dick, with his usual zeal to account for every waking moment, arranges a precise itinerary with a travel agency, but somehow in total variance with his usual custom and to my delight, he's also arranged a car rental. By ourselves, he tells me, we'll motor from Paris, through the Rhône valley and the chateau region, all the way down to Nice. Dick speaks French; I speak a little, so between us and a good road map, he figures we'll be able to arrive each night at the destination the travel agent has booked for us.

Paris is all that Paris is supposed to be. My uncle, Austin Purves, my father's brother and a well-known artist, is creating a war memorial, commissioned by the French government, a mosaic Pieta honoring the WWII Americans killed fighting on French soil. Instead of the dead Christ, the grieving Madonna will hold a dead GI in her lap. My uncle has rented an atelier in Paris and is assembling the Pieta with the help of two craftsmen who work in mosaic. Great sheets of brown paper with the figures sketched in charcoal have been mailed from his studio in Litchfield, Connecticut, and are now spread out on the floor awaiting the mosaic squares. The squares have to be glued onto the brown paper sketches, back side to, and mirror fashion. Later, the brown paper with its glued mosaic pieces will be shipped to Draguignon, there pressed into wet cement, the brown paper peeled off and voila! The figures emerge from their mirror mode, right side up and right side to.*

---

* The ability to see mirror-fashion is an Asperger's trait.

"What if you make a mistake?" I ask my uncle.

"You have to take a pickaxe to the cement."

Dick enjoys all this, including an evening ride up the Seine in the Bateau Mouche, Uncle Austin and Aunt Ellen, Dick and I, all four of us singing at the top of our lungs. The next day in our rented car, we drive out of Paris and into the French countryside with its mackerel skies and wheat fields bordered with the flowers that wreathe little girls' straw hats: daisies, buttercups, corn flowers, and poppies. Released from the strain of autism, Dick sheds his anxiety, and we throw away the travel agent's itinerary. We drive off on an unplanned side trip into the fringes of the Alps, spend a night with a troop of hikers, share supper with them at a long trestle table and carry on in broken French.

When we finally reach Nice, it's a startling disappointment. The stretch of pebbles that passes for a beach reeks of French perfume and sweat. Scrawny codgers, their withered loins ill-covered, totter about, ogling girls.

Now really throwing away the itinerary, we get back in the car to motor away the afternoon looping up and down and along and around the winding roads of the Riviera coast. Finally we come to an inn entrance that looks vaguely impressive, drive up and book a room, only to realize that by some miracle of beginner's luck, we've found our way to Noel Coward land: the Hotel du Cap in Cap D'Antibes. The long and short of it is we end up cruising the Riviera with a couple from Chile who've chartered a boat out of Cannes and ask us to join them. Dick says yes and, for once in his life, enjoys improvising. We rove the Mediterranean, anchor off tiny islands known only to boats that can moor in shallow water, and sail to St. Tropez, already a destination for the great and glamorous but as yet untouched by hype.

Dick's purchase a year later of a cabin cruiser for the Vineyard harks back, I feel sure, to this European trip. A recollection of total happiness.

Chapter 4

The Separate Worlds Begin

It's late summer and we're back in Dedham from the Vineyard. Temple's turned seven, and family life has settled into a routine. I should have a sense of achievement, but, instead, I feel anxious and empty, longing for the old beckon and wink of Cambridge. I watch the children playing in the field behind our house and into my consciousness slides a recollection of myself at Temple's age.

I'm exploring with my cousin on a golden afternoon like this one, pleased beyond words that he's allowed me to tag along. We've climbed the stairs to a little windowed tower at the top of a once beautiful summer mansion, now abandoned and boarded up, a white elephant brought low by the Depression. Already we've roamed the peeling main floor: drawing room, dining room, butler's pantry, kitchen, back pantry, and maids' dining room. Up the grand front stairs to the second floor expanse of master bedrooms; then to the third, where the floorboards of the maids' rooms squeak under our sneakers, scaring us silly. We brace ourselves, ready to run in case there's a caretaker, praying it'll be a caretaker and not a ghost lurking in these last shadowy rooms where cracks of sunshine beam through the broken window shutters. The house entices us up one last staircase, steps no wider than our feet and steep as a ladder.

Up we climb to a hot little turret, bright with sun and hung with spider webs long deserted by their spinners. We peer out the smudged turret windows and there, spread below us, is our countryside dusted with Queen Anne's Lace: fields, hilltop, stables—all of it made strange from this wild height. On the turret window ledge is a wooden box with a glass cover; in it, nesting on wads of sun-yellowed cotton, a collection of blown bird eggs. Had they once belonged to some boy? Did he lose interest and leave them to the spiders? Carefully, we take out the eggs one by one, light as air, with their tiny pinprick holes at each end. The last egg gives out a papery thud when we shake it. Unable to bear not knowing, we crack it open and inside is the dried mummy of a baby bird.

Why now, twenty years later, do I remember the touch of that tiny mummy, brittle as the ancient flies upside down on the window ledge—flies that once bumped against the hot dusty windows, believing that because they could see the sun they could escape to it? Am I doomed like the bird mummy never to hatch, left to dry up in an empty tower room, turned to nothing but a papery thud inside a shell? I must make something happen, make life wink and beckon again. If I lose track of my own life, how can I coax Temple to look for hers? Temple is in school all day now. Though I can't take on a full-time job, I can make the free afternoon hours count.

Everybody ought to have a tacky dream to start off with. Nothing distinguished like wanting to be Mrs. Roosevelt or Lena Horne, just a dream to get going. If anyone calls you dumb for wanting a Flokati rug or a rip-off copy of a Dior suit, tell them distinction will come later.

My tacky dream is film noir: a grade B movie dream, laid in cheap smoke-filled nightclub with me as the girl singer—but let me lead up to it.

I begin by singing in the afternoon for the Elks, I can't remember exactly how I got there: something to do with the man in charge of putting on shows for hospital vets. He confuses my performance in the Vincent Club with the St. Vincent de Paul Society. The Vincent Club is an old Boston institution that puts on the female equivalent of Harvard's Hasty Pudding Show in order to raise money for the Vincent Memorial Hospital (part of the Massachusetts General). It's an honor to be in it, and the show's run is a social plum. All this is too complicated to explain to the Elks' man, and who am I to argue with him when he's beckoning me in?

"Sure you can sing for us, I know you St. Vincent girls. You're all right." I sing him a calypso song in the auditorium of a veterans' hospital. Very nervous, very bad, but the nurses applaud. Anything to break the monotony.

The Elks' man sets me up with a guitar player and puts us to working the vet wards where the wounded from the Korean War are being stitched back together again.

I soon learn that every ward has a "card"; he's the guy who leads the other guys into joking. Find the card, joke with him, and the rest of the ward will get behind you—or him, depending on how the jokes go. Then find the shyest boy in the ward, sit on his bed and sing, "Let Me Call You Sweetheart."

The guitar player and I move from ward to ward. Sometimes he plays for me; sometimes he sings his own songs like "Who'll Bite Your Neck When I Am Old, Dear, After My Teeth Are Gone?" In one ward the card turns out to be an elderly vet who lies flat on his back like an overturned turtle. Paralyzed since WWI, stretched out on a slanted bed board, he's been looking out the same window at the same sunset for almost forty years now. The men love him. "He's the greatest," they tell me. "Always laughing."

No one warns me about the handful of men whose faces have been shot off. Nor about the locked wards for vets who've lost their minds. They leave their mark, those men; you don't forget them.

Meanwhile, far away in another galaxy, Temple continues to thrive.

Next, I study piano with Nappy Gagnon, who plays for acts in a Boston nightclub and teaches me pop chording. I tell Nappy I want to learn to play be-bop.

"You'll have to play more Bach; all bop is based on Bach." I remember that Bach was what Temple hummed before she could speak. It was how I knew her hearing wasn't scrambled, that she was taking in the notes I was playing.

Along with playing two- and three-part inventions, I study legitimate voice with Dr. Wadsworth Provandie, pour German lieder and French art songs into my soul, wash them down with blues, jazz, and the sobbing cry of Edith Piaf, the "sparrow" of postwar Paris. I learn pop singing from Ray Dorey, a local radio star. Ray always opens his radio show with the words, "Good morning, this is Mrs. Dorey's boy, Ray," and closes it singing, "It's a Big, Wide, Wonderful World We Live In." Ray, who's been a top band vocalist, teaches me how to phrase with the music.

"Let go the note. Even if the sheet music is marked to hold it, let go and let the music breathe around you."

I catch onto the knack and find that song phrasing is like sailing in a little knockabout. Again I'm back in my childhood with my cousin, sailing with him in *The Golden Eye*. He's teaching me how to tack close-hauled: "See the dark water up ahead? That's the wind coming. As soon as the dark hits the bow, head the boat up into the wind, and we'll go fast."

I do and the old knockabout lifts on the wind puff, her bow rising up out of the water.

So that's pop phrasing? The singer steers the boat, keeps the lyrics close-hauled; the band improvises, and the song rides on the beat? I learn to feel it, as long ago I felt *The Golden Eye* lift out of the water.

Pop singing turns me on to jazz—new and old; I listen to it at every chance. The Huntington Avenue music store allows customers to play a record before committing to its purchase. I sit in one of their glass-doored booths listening to Dixieland and boogie-woogie 78s, newly reissued on long-playing 33s, avidly reading the jazz histories printed on their shiny new LP covers. The store clerk doesn't seem to care; he doesn't pound on the glass door asking me do I really intend to buy or am I freeloading. I'm freeloading, of course, but so's everybody else.

George Wein has taken over an old nightspot and is presenting the jazz greats. One after another they make their appearance: Art Tatum, George Shearing, Oscar Peterson, Louis Armstrong, Ethel Waters—they're all turning up there. One week it's Pee Wee Russell. Pee Wee is a clarinet player from the twenties whose music I love.

Dick declines to go, so I find myself sitting alone on a worn vinyl banquette, staring at the cracked black walls of Wein's nightclub, now adorned with white Steinberg-style line sketches of New Orleans jazzmen—in particular, one noted in Dixieland for playing the slide trombone with his toes.

From the tiny bandstand George Wein introduces Pee Wee Russell. The response is scattered. Pee Wee's name rings no bell with the young, hip crowd, too cool for the ebullience of Dixieland, preferring the mellow intricacies of the Modern Jazz Quartet. Pee Wee mounts the bandstand, his tall, skinny frame unsteady from an overdose of booze. He makes stabs at his mouth with his clarinet, but can't seem to connect it to his lips.

The crowd watches, nudges, whispers. Somebody guffaws. The guffaw does it. In a flash George Wein is back up on the stand.

"Don't you dare laugh. You don't know anything about this man. He's a musical great."

The tough scold works. The crowd quiets. Pee Wee straightens, connects his clarinet with his mouth and plays a haunting riff. Another effort at sobriety, and he launches into a slow number, segues to a second slow number and then takes a break. The crowd applauds, polite but unimpressed.

Then, mysteriously, a message comes up to the bandstand: Lennie would like to play the blues with Pee Wee. From the banquette darkness, pushing his way through the drink tables comes Leonard Bernstein, already a towering musical figure, Kousevitsky's protégé conductor of the Boston Symphony Orchestra. He sits down at the piano and nods at Pee Wee. Pee Wee straightens, gives a courtly bow and plays a ribbon of melody. Lennie echoes it on the piano, punctuates it with an invention of his own. Pee Wee repeats Lennie's phrase. Piano and clarinet begin to twine around each other. Over and over, Lennie woos the blues out of the old star until they sing as one—young Lennie on the up and up, swaying over the piano, and long string bean Pee Wee hunched over the last days of his clarinet.

The cool crowd goes wild.

The Dedham neighborhood young have accepted Temple into the "Wampatuck Gang." The Wampatuck Gang consists of all the children who live on Wampatuck Circle, the semi-circular road bounded by our street, Lowder Street. On the other side of Lowder Street is a stone wall marking off a small farm, an open field, and a scrub wood hiding a large estate. In the children's nursery years, we've breakfasted to the crow of Mr. Brown's rooster, crossed Lowder Street, and watched Mr. Brown harness up his workhorse to plow the field for a vegetable patch. Then we've watched his hens descend from the henhouse, look at us sideways, duck their heads and pick their way down the little wooden ramp like a gaggle of disapproving ladies coming out of church. But now, the children have outgrown the simple joys of Beatrix Potter; they've seen me in a Vincent Show, and the theatre bug has taken over. They've turned their bedroom into a stage, constructed cardboard scenery, and rigged up a sheet for a curtain. Plots are makeshift; starring roles are what count. Temple plays "Bizban." Bizban is Temple's imaginary playmate who carries out the pranks she longs to do but has been warned off by her caution gene. Her best friend, Lyman (of Crusader Mouse fame), has no such compunction, seeing in Temple's "Bizban" performance a possible partner for real life mischief. The two soon sic each other into pranks that Temple won't admit to until it's all over, happy to scare me later with her renegade gene. The few times she and Lyman are caught, their deeds turn out to be not so much bad as pesky, outside the line but not very far. Temple's basic good sense and Lyman's smile—he looks like Dennis the Menace—work in combination. Just pray they don't fall out of a tree like a pair of baby robins and break their necks.

And me? How does my renegade gene play out?

An agent calls, offering me a singing gig in a cheap nightspot. The odd thing is, Dick seems rather proud, that is, until he hears a number of pursed-lipped comments circulating among the more conservative of the Leave-it-to-Beaver world. Caught off guard, he mounts the stump and starts in on me. Bad enough, he shouts, to have an unacceptable daughter. Now he has two unacceptables: a child who can't behave and a wife who won't!

"Why shouldn't I sing?" I protest. "The job is at night, after the kids have gone to bed. I'm a good singer; I've worked hard for it."

"It isn't work. You like singing."

"Work is something you don't like?"

The tight little man in Dick's brain can't figure that one. Stopping me is all he can deal with. "You've had your way with Temple. That should be enough for you."

"I've already signed the contract."

"You can't do it! Everybody says so."

"How do you know you don't say so, then everybody mumbles a vague 'yes' to you, just to be neighborly?"

Dick gnaws his cheek and stares out the window.

Freed from their Sunday clothes, the Wampatuck Gang is running loose in the open field, floating banners that read "Bizban Forever." In a barking circle around them are the Wampatuck dogs and a large white duck named Wilhemina, given as a downy yellow Easter present to Neddy, another neighborhood boy. Wilhemina has survived the holiday mauling and grown into a handsome white duck. Snubbed by the hens, who won't let her into Mr. Brown's coop, she's now decided to be a dog. To everyone's amazement, the dogs have accepted her.

"Only Hal Roach could dream up Wilhemina."

Dick is too single-minded to be entertained by my quip. "The only reason that cheap club hires you is because your picture was all over the paper after you sang in the Vincent Show. And the Vincent Club loved it! It sold tickets."

Before I can answer, Dick has strapped on his back brace and gone out to mow the front lawn. Back and forth, back and forth, brow furrowed, shoulders hunched, he cuts angry swathes through the lush new green, furious at June's ebullience.

He's feeling tricked. His sister has told me that he's complained to her that I keep setting up new rules, and then, "Dammit all, it turns out she's right!" Sort of a backhanded compliment, why does it always have to be, "Dammit all?"

The lawn done, Dick spreads fertilizer. God knows the lawn doesn't need it now, but if he doesn't feed it, the summer heat will kill it off. Always a feast or a famine, eh Dick? Nothing stays put, including me.

Dick studies the bare patches on the driveway where the snow-plow has shoveled up the gravel. Dandelions and witchgrass are already springing up. Tar will be his answer. He'll call it a capital investment.

He puts away the lawn mower, heads for his desk and the pile of financial figures spread out beside his adding machine. How he loves that adding machine, the sound of it, the long white curl of paper. "You know where you stand with an adding machine." That's his favorite remark. The same goes for his boat. "You can count on a boat. It holds to a course. And boat chores, once you've done them, they stay done. The boat's good for Temple, too."

I don't deny that.

"She likes polishing the boat brass. None of that giggling and spitting on the boat."

What's really upset Dick is his sister's teasing him about Jep.

"Who's Jep?" the children chorus. Dick's sister laughs.

"Jep's the imaginary collie your father had as a little boy. Jep lived under the sofa."

Dick turns red and laughs too. "Don't," he begs his sister. Too late. Jep's escaped from under the sofa, and Dick can't stop laughing. Shamefaced, a little out of control, he laughs like Temple when she laughs about Bizban. Like Temple, he can't seem to make the laughter stop. Is Jep the reason for his fierce conviction that life and laughter, like the June grass, will get the better of him if he doesn't mow it down?

After supper I sing to him. "Blue Moon, you saw me standing alone." It's his favorite song.

"You can sing, that's the bitch of it. Something in your voice, in the song. God, a pop song can break your heart." Later that evening I find a letter on my side of the bed, a true love letter, the first he's ever composed.

"I can't bear to think of you standing alone," he's written, quoting the lyric of the song. "You're the one I want to be there for. Someone you really could care for."

My fantasy is to be the girl singer in a cheap joint in a Grade B detective movie, singing "Blue Moon" to Dick.

I take the gig and turn up at the club the afternoon of my opening night. I introduce myself to the piano player, who's Irish and friendly, and to the comic, who's setting up music cues with him. The comic stares, snorts, and goes back to his cues. Instead of waiting my turn, I stand by the piano and gush at both of them. I can't seem to stop; my tongue's gone crazy with excitement. After the piano rehearsal, I find my way to my dressing room and hang up my gowns. The phone rings.

"I'm the rep from AGVA." It's a hoarse male voice. "You can't go on till you've paid your dues." Dues to what? What's he talking about? "You debutantes, you think you can get away with murder." Murder? "Who's your agent?"

"Al Navarro."

"Al knows better than to pull this. He knows we don't take it down at AGVA. We're a respectable, high class union." He goes into a long garbled harangue about union honor and cheating. He does all the talking, which is lucky because I haven't a clue what he's yelling about.

"I'll call Al," I offer.

"No. I'll call him. You're young. You don't know nothin'. Al knows better. He's gonna hear from me."

As soon as he hangs up, I call Al. He laughs.

"Let me deal with him. Stay in your room till it's time to go on."

This is all so exciting I can hardly bear it. I'm really, truly in the middle of a Grade B movie. I squeeze into my black satin gown, so tight I can't sit in it, and mince down the stairs. The comic watches me from the bottom of the stairs and sucks his teeth. I explain to him that I have to mince; it's the only way I can negotiate in the gown. The comic gives his racing form a snap.

"We're working for a guy named Harry Hess. He don't know his Hess from a hole in the wall."

I giggle. He snaps my garter.

"You can't do that."

"I already did." The comic's name is Leon. I know because, outside the club, for all of Huntington Avenue to see, are five-foot high advertising blow-ups of the two of us. My mother has already driven by and, in her shock, arranged to be out of town.

Harry Hess emerges from the bar, pushing ahead of him the AGVA rep, a shrunken relic from vaudeville, now thoroughly cowed by Hess, Hess's lugubrious face, his pink-tinted glasses, his heavy prompting paw. The rep gulps, runs his fingers round his stained hat brim.

"It was not my intention to upset you, Miss. I know what it's like to break in a new act. I know how the nerves can play games. I wouldn't want to upset a nice young lady like you."

Hess grunts approval. The rep tries to get his hat back on at a jaunty angle, but Hess pushes him out the door. The rep hurries down the steps. Hess looks at me. "Yeah, you're a nice kid, but your act stinks. Forget them ballads you're rehearsing. Stick to the jump tunes."

Hess has hired a blonde to sing the ballads. The blonde's name is Dana and when she isn't doing her act, she wears a fluffy angora stole snuggled round her shoulders—not really a sweater, more of an imitation fur. Or, maybe, a negligee. Will I ever be able to sing ballads and wear something like that? My gown is black satin, but my no-nonsense face gives me away. Dana's gown is white satin, cut on the bias. Her ballads are slow and sensuous.

"I'd work for you. I'd slave for you. I'd be a beggar or a knave for you." She strokes her thighs as she sings. "If that isn't love, it'll have to do…" No wonder Hess wants me to stick to the jump tunes.

Leon is at my side. "Every time I meet a girl I like, either she's married or I am." Leon needs someone to fire off jokes to, so he can warm up his act. I give him a giggle. Leon runs up onto the bandstand, flashes his diamond pinkie ring in the spot, and starts in. "My gall stones! I had 'em mounted." From there, he goes into a Charles Laughton/Quasimodo routine. Hess stands at the back of the room and growls.

"That's in very bad taste. There could be customers here with a cripple in the family. He could be hurting their feelings." I have trouble making the connection, but by the time I've thought of an answer, Hess has left to do business in the bar. There seems to be a lot of business in the bar, a lot of coming and going, heavy on the cash register, not a whole lot on the drinks.

"They're making book. We're the front for it." It's Leon. He's come off the stand, and the tenor is singing now. "That jerk should be selling neckties at Woolworths." Leon lopes back up to the mike and talks the tenor into letting him into his act. He tells the tenor to put his arms behind his back. Leon will be his arms. The tenor does what Leon tells him and the result is hilarious, particularly since the tenor can't see what Leon's up to and is dumb enough to think he's the reason for the applause. Leon comes off the stand and winks at me. Hess storms out of the bar.

"That's very low class!" He's furious I'm laughing. "Get up there and sing 'La Vie en Rose'. Dana don't do French." Hess is impressed I can sing in French. "I got a newspaper columnist in the bar. He's ready to write a story on us. So, after you sing "La Vie en Rose," sing "The Lady is a Tramp" and when you get to the line 'I follow Winchell,' put in the columnist's name." I do.

After I come off the stand, the columnist introduces himself and his wife. "Thanks for the plug."

I babble at him that I read his column every day, which is a great thumping lie. He smirks anyway.

"You're a nice kid, but your act stinks. Lay off the jump tunes. Stick to the ballads."

The next night, the columnist turns up alone. And drunk.

"Sing 'La Vie en Rose'," he calls out. I do, and a customer talks through it, which I'm used to, but the columnist isn't. Not tonight anyway. Tonight, he is my defender. He rises unsteadily and wags his finger. "Nobody talks when she sings, you sonovabitch."

The talking customer rises, also unsteady and twice the size of the columnist.

"Nobody calls me a sonovabitch, you sonovabitch."

I feel somehow responsible, and sing all the verses to "La Vie en Rose." The two men lumber toward each other, leaving a wake of kicked-over chairs. Nervous patrons pay and run; others grin and watch. A waiter goes for Hess. My caution goes into alert. It's a grade B movie all right, but who's scripting it? I mince off the bandstand and, as soon as I'm out of sight, pull my black satin dress up over my knees, sprint up the stairs to my dressing room, yank it off, pull on my suburban sweater and skirt, run out, find my car, and speed home to the safety of my suburban identity.

The next night, Hess joins me while I'm waiting to go on.

"You get home all right?"

"Sure."

Hess has the columnist on his mind. "We get him outta the room. Soon as he comes into the bar, he starts in abusing me. I get the bartender and we shove him out the door. Next thing I know, he's laying in the gutter." For the first time Hess seems off his game. "I don't want to leave him laying there. I don't want to call the cops. So I call the other clubs. They all say 'not to worry.' He's done it lots."

Meaning the booze.

"I don't want to call the cops, see, 'cause he got a name in this town. He could ruin me."

Meaning the bookie business.

But nothing comes of it, and nothing turns up in the newspaper column good or bad, which is just as well. The gig's over, and I don't need to see my renegade gene in print.

"Thanks for the job, Hess."

Hess nods, turns his attention to Leon who's pretending to take out his glass eye, blow on it, polish it on his lapel, and put it back in. There's a bored clinking of ice cubes. Hess frowns.

"You know something?" he says to me. "One of these days I'm gonna open a real lounge, a 'class' room. Somewhere's out in

Brookline, and I'm going to be calling you. You know why? 'Cause you can talk." Meaning my patter between songs. Hess is the first person to believe in my words, to think perhaps there might even be money in them. But he doesn't call, so I never learn if he gets his "room."

We shake hands to say goodbye. I don't tell Hess about the chair in my dressing room that Dick has smashed in a rage.

As well as performing in the Vincent Show, I take on running it, a substantial production task since the cast numbers around fifty. However, because I have a great crew, I can cover a good portion of the work from home. The director—who the next year will be hired by the Metropolitan impresario, Rudolf Bing, to be his right hand man—teaches me stagecraft. Everything I'm learning, he says, will apply for any stage production.

Because I'm in charge, Temple and her sister are given the honor of coming up on stage and drawing lucky numbers for prizes donated by the Boston stores. Dressed in their best, complete to scratchy petticoats, the two little girls find being up on a big stage more exciting than being down in the audience. I peep at them from the wings, knowing that home plays will increase in length, style, and insistence that I be there to applaud.

Meanwhile, between performances, a reporter from the *Boston Globe* turns up to interview me. Nervous from the newspaper press over my bookie joint gig, I tell him he can only talk to me for ten minutes, but we hit it off, and the ten minutes stretch into an hour. That night, after seeing the show, he admits he's Lyon Phelps, the nephew of Yale's William Lyon Phelps, and the playwright president of the Poets Theatre in Cambridge. Would I be willing to take part in a Poets Theatre reading?

You bet.

The play, *A Leak in the Universe*, turns out to be by the eminent Harvard professor and poet, I.A. Richards, and I am to read opposite Dr. Richards himself. The reading is held in Alice James' Cambridge drawing room before a small and unbelievably distinguished audience: Harvard President Nathan Pusey, actor Walter Abel, and a covey of Harvard's top professors—all friends of Dr. Richards. Fortunately, because of the spotlights imported for the reading, I'm blind to their distinction until the reading is finished. Afterwards, the director asks me if I'd consider performing in a full Poets Theatre production.

Awed, I say yes. This is my real dream.

The Poets Theatre, literally a theatre for poets, is producing the dramatic work of America's best: Mary Manning, Sylvia Plath, Ted Hughes, Anne Sexton, James Merrill, Richard Wilbur, Frank O'Hara, and V.R. Lang. Under the theatre's auspices, Dylan Thomas has already given his first American reading, and Truman Capote will shortly take Cambridge by storm reading from an unpublished manuscript.

"I'm going to read you a story I just wrote," he'll tell the audience. "It's about a girl named Holly Golightly."

Realizing the importance of this theatre, knowing that I can't swing a full-time job, I parcel out my free time carefully and help out with production.

My first production assignment is for Ionesco's play, *The Bald Soprano*, newly translated into English by Donald Allen. It's a brilliant, stylish piece performed in black and white, the actors' faces whitened, then a black line drawn down the center of each. The reviewers scorn it. "The Poets Theatre has lost its mind," the newspapers trumpet, not knowing how soon the play will become a classic, taught in every English department.

While working on production, I accept the amused snubs of the poetry crowd who think that, because I don't react to their snubs, I don't understand them. It doesn't matter. Their poetry nourishes me anyway, and I'm too impressed by their Olympian talents to dare to aspire to the password into their world. Besides, some of them aren't too sure of the password either, so they certainly can't afford to talk to me. If we do talk, my vocabulary, which Dick scorns as over-elaborate, becomes a blur of smiling stammers. Though I'm pregnant again, I continue to work on production, not wanting to lose the connection.

One of the poets arranges to have Dame Edith and Sir Osbert Sitwell give a poetry reading in Sanders Theatre, which seats over a thousand people. A literary honor for the Poets Theatre and potential financial boon, the little theatre on Palmer Street is in need of a new toilet. Mary Manning, the theatre's guiding light, remarks, "Perhaps this will pay for both a sit well and a stand well."

The theatre can't afford any advertising, and for some reason I can't fully fathom, I'm handed the task of arranging press releases. Not wanting to admit my ignorance, desperate for some kind of know-how, I go to Alison Arnold, Society Editor for the Boston Herald. As soon as Mrs. Arnold learns the nature of my assignment, she sits me down in her office and teaches me how to write a press release. (Lord, people are kind!)

"Give each paper a little different story. Don't release all your information to one paper because, once they print it, it becomes dead news and the other papers won't touch it."

I do as she bids, and the press, thrilled at the possibility of compiling their own Sitwell story, ask for a press conference.

A press conference? I hadn't figured on that, nor had the Poets Theatre, which had but ten dollars in the till. I take the ten dollars and a deep breath. Great with my fourth child, I head for The Ritz Carlton Hotel where I'm told the Sitwells will be staying. I explain my problem to the major domo of The Ritz Carlton dining room who looks at my ten dollars and bursts out laughing.

"That won't buy you two drinks in the bar."

I must have looked crestfallen.

"Tell you what you can do. The Sitwells have a private suite, so your press conference can come under the heading of a private party instead of a function you'd have to pay the hotel for. Take your ten dollars, buy some whiskey and crackers and cheese (ten dollars went further in those days). Pack it all into a suitcase, walk through the lobby as inconspicuously as possible, take the elevator to the Sitwell's floor, and give the suitcase to Joe. Meanwhile, I'll tell Joe you're coming, and he'll set up a serving table. If you can find your way to giving Joe a couple of dollars, it wouldn't be a bad idea."

Again, I do as I'm told and again it works. Before the press arrives—and they do arrive, every one of them—the Sitwells welcome me like a favorite niece. Sir Osbert, ever gallant, helps me off with my coat but is suffering from the early stages of Parkinson's so he can't get the coat onto a hanger. After a humiliating struggle, he thrusts both the coat and the hanger out to me.

"Here, you do it. This damn disease drives me crazy."

Dame Edith, arrayed in a long robe and richly embroidered headpiece, arranges herself on a sofa looking for all the world like a Beardsley sorceress. I can't take my eyes off her long, thin fingers adorned with mammoth aquamarines.

I don't remember how it comes about, but before the press arrives, we strike up a conversation about ghosts, and I learn that Sir Osbert was friends with M. R. James, the Edwardian writer of ghost stories.

"Is *Canon Alberic's Scrapbook* true?" I ask.

"Well, I think Mickey thought it was true after he'd told it," says Sir Osbert.

At noon the press arrives and Joe, in a white jacket, manages to make my $10 outlay of booze and crackers look like a catered spread. The press, too impressed to drink, stare at the Sitwells and ask questions that have nothing to do with poetry—like what size shoe does Dame Edith wear. Dame Edith, whose feet are as long as her fingers, stares at their feet and replies coolly, "American women have feet like buns."

When it's all over, Joe packs my suitcase with the unopened whiskey, which I promptly return to the local liquor store. The whole affair, including Joe's tip, comes to $11.65, the extra $1.65 due to a teetotaling reporter from the *Christian Science Monitor* who ordered ginger ale from room service.

Because of all the press—including an article by Alison Arnold—all one thousand, one hundred and sixty-five seats in Sanders Theatre sell out.

The night of the reading, the stage is decorated with blossoming trees left over from the Spring Flower Show. The Sitwells sit under them in a pair of needlepoint armchairs. Two richly embellished icons. Pre-Raphaelite, yes, but reincarnated by Gilbert and Sullivan:

"Walk down Picadilly with a poppy or a lily in your medieval hand."

Anne Sexton's poetry reading—no such grand affair as the Sitwells'—is a private Sunday afternoon gathering in the forty-seat Palmer Street theatre. It's Sexton's first reading since her nervous breakdown. Pretty and touchingly ill at ease, she reads poems she's written during her breakdown, summoning with lyric genius the suffocating trap of suburbia, which fits too tight and is squeezing the life out of her. Her husband sits nearby, guarding her tenderly, but in the end it will not be enough.

June 1955. My fourth child is born, a baby girl, healthy in every respect, save for nightly bouts of colic. The colic pains strike her every evening between six and nine o'clock and with them come her decibel screams. I rush to the bassinet. Tears and infant drooling have already soaked the diaper under her, leaving her face and knees raw. I feel her tiny abdomen; it's swollen hard. Tight as a drum—that's colic, all right. I wrap a blanket round her, put her up my shoulder; and the vertical position gives instant relief. The drum belly lets go; her baby screams subside into gulps. Exhausted, she nuzzles into my neck, falls asleep on my shoulder, and together we watch the *Milton Berle Show*.

Six months later, Temple's sister again takes charge. This time, since the baby's a girl, baths are only the first step. After the bath comes choosing what the baby should wear, followed by an overlay of adornment. Beads, broaches, earrings, bracelets, scarves and headbands are draped over and around the baby until she looks like a miniature version of Dame Edith Sitwell. Needless to say, the baby loves it.

Four months after the baby's birth, I'm cast as Célimène in a Poets Theatre premiere: Richard Wilbur's verse translation of Molière's: *The Misanthrope.* Célimène, so utterly sure of herself, so at home with the wiles of 17th century court life, is the antithesis of me; and Wilbur's elegant couplets, rhymed as Molière rhymed his, are in total contrast to my own daily speech patterns. I find Célimène's character a dramatic challenge, even a challenge to speak in Wilbur's rhymed couplets without letting them jingle. But that's only part of my problems.

"Take your thumbs out of your fists," the director orders. "It's a sign of dependence."

Really?

"Yes, you must learn to act with enthusiasm. Do you know what the word means?" I thought I did, but it's clear I don't.

"It means 'in *theos.*' With the God spirit in you." The director looks over the rest of me. "Lose ten pounds, and, face it right now: you can never act again without a girdle."

The costume designer creates a ravishing costume for me of peach-colored satin. The embroidery painted on it is so perfect, one could almost take it for the real thing. We get into costume next door in Morris Pancoast's antique shop, a Collyer Brothers' jumble of Morris' oil paintings, heaped together with broken rocking chairs and bureaus with no drawer pulls and whatever else Morris still dreams of selling. One performance night, while putting on a pair of antique gold and pearl earrings, I drop one and have to grope through inches of furry dust before I can find it.

The play opens, and Richard Wilbur wins accolades. Leonard Bernstein and Lillian Hellman come to see it and immediately approach Wilbur to write the lyrics for their new work-in-progress based on Voltaire's *Candide*, destined to become a musical classic.

At the time of *The Misanthrope*, neither Richard Wilbur nor I had any idea that the other had an autistic child. It wasn't something you talked about in 1955.

Years from now, while studying acting in New York, I'll learn how to use empathy and sensory recollection as ways to identify more effectively with a stage character like Célimène. In the process, I'll catch my first glimpse into what an autistic person is missing emotionally. That glimpse will, in time, guide me to a fuller exploration of autism.

Sort of like traveling up the Nile to find its source.

It's June and the Vineyard is in its blossoming glory. Every beach plum, privet hedge, mock orange, and lilac is putting forth an extravagant array of blooms.

The nanny has long since departed and a pair of Irish girls has joined our household. They teach us how to play Camogie.

"It's a kind of field hockey. We've a cousin who'll make us the Camogie sticks so we can play it right out front here."

The siblings adore the Irish girls. "They're like older sisters to us." *

Somewhere in the long summer stretches, I develop two family passwords. The first is a direct command which goes: "This is what we're going to do. Do you want it nice or do you want it cross? I'd be happy to do it either way." The children know it means there's no room to bargain. The other is, "We'll see." That means, "I hear you, and I'm thinking about it, but if you whine and wheedle, I'll get cross and say no." "We'll see" requires obedient nods followed by diplomatic circling, preferably in the form of jokes. The siblings, knowing I'm a sucker for a laugh, soon learn that, if they entertain me with their wants they stand a better chance of getting them.

It's Temple's first encounter with humor.

Temple's younger sister, already a gifted little actress, longs to perform in something more advanced than a school play. We decide to stage another Molière work, *The Imaginary Invalid*, and cast it with other talented neighborhood children. As the play takes shape, I see that the three lead children are indeed exceptional and deserve first-rate costumes. A quick trip up to a costume house outside Boston and we have elegant miniature 17th century costumes. A local antique store lends us a chandelier, and our neighbor, Dr. Henri Peyre, head of the Romance Language Department at Yale, offers to introduce the play. He's enchanted with Temple's sister's performance.

"That little monkey," he says, bending double with laughter. "She is so funny, so talented."

---

* Dear Irish sisters: If you should come upon these words, know that we all think of you and get in touch.

Temple isn't quite sure what it is her sister does that makes her funny, only that it produces laughter, and she'd like to do that too.

"I want to be in the play, I really, really want to be in it," she pleads.

"If I let you be in it, will you remember that the play is for your sister, not for you?"

"Yes, yes, I know."

"One false move and I'll kill you. Do you understand? The siblings will kill you, too."

"I understand, I really understand, I really, really, really want to do it." She sashays around me, almost catching the drift of what goes into the making of a joke and a performance.

She does perform in the play, not with the style of the others, but she manages to learn her lines, follow stage directions, and hold up her end of the bargain.

I miss those Vineyard summers, yearn for them as for no other place in time. Years later, when I return to the Vineyard and look out on the blue Sound with its scattered wisps of sail boats, when I listen again for the familiar thud of the ferry, I'll be there and not there. The familiar will have grown odd, as Rip Van Winkle discovered when he finally woke up. I'll drive past my old house, a huge Victorian summer camp with porches wide enough to ride a tricycle on, with three floors and fourteen beds—one of them still painted either red or a bilious salmon depending on which side of it you're looking at—with a dining table big enough for ping-pong, and a sandy path leading through the scrub oaks and trumpet vine, beach roses and honeysuckle, down across a pebbly beach to a splintery dock, its barnacled piles bearded with brown seaweed where minnows dart.

Chapter 4 - The Separate Worlds Begin

The pier is gone, and, when I look up from the beach, I see that my house has been stripped of its scrub oaks and stands exposed on a carpet of imported sod, edged with hydrangeas. The battered screen door has been given a portico, the porch painted a blazing white and monogrammed with a wooden whale. The old matriarch, whose weathered shingles held us together for so many summers, is now buffed and bedizened beyond recognition.

The past, my beloved past, that time and place when we were all happy, where battles over Temple disappeared, and Dick and I found our way to a brief harmony. A handful of halcyon years before Dick lost his real estate job and his precarious emotional footing.

Chapter 5

Things Fall Apart

The Boston ethos is not always friendly. Early on, the Boston fathers laid it out: "To work is to pray," they said, and setting to with it, found their prayers answered with industrial bounty. Contrary to the Biblical notion of "love thy neighbor," such bounty led to self-interest and meanness of character, which surprised the fathers but was too good to stop. Soon, every river, every babbling brook was harnessed to a mill factory, where there was plenty of fourteen-hour-a-day labor for the impoverished immigrants pouring into New England. If the immigrants remained impoverished, the fathers said it was because they were godless and lazy.

The old Puritan prayer continued to produce income, but the income was moved into investment firms where it was less visible. Money and self-interest went unspoken like a facial mole; distinction was the new order of the day. The mill owners now sent their sons to Harvard, not to study for the ministry but to acquire an intellectual polish equal to that of Europe. Boston became the Athens of America.

However, there were then and always will be Boston scions who lack the acumen or fortune to make it into the ranks of the distinguished. Such a one was a small, mean man who'd spent his youth as a gentleman jockey and now sold real estate. Why he chose to woo Dick away from the real estate company Dick was working for and into his company, I have no idea. Somehow the two men impressed each other and Dick signed on.

Before the winter was over, Dick came home to blurt out a garbled tale of woe. Knowing Dick, he must have played a part in it, but I put most of the blame on the Puritan meanness-of-character trait. No doubt the little man hated his own hard-bitten jockey face, his skinny jockey frame, his career of non-distinction-flaws I'm sure his Yankee family had been quick to point out. A fight with a man of his own social rank, a handsome man who was bigger and more charming than he, but a man he could taunt and still keep the advantage, was a way to get back a bit of his own. Dick had never had to answer for his temper as Temple was learning to answer for hers. In confrontation with a man whose family he admired, anxiety must have triggered his rage, and for that the man made him pay the price. He broke Dick as easily as a bully breaks a terrier with a rolled up newspaper.

"He fired me. We had a fight and I lost my temper." In a state of total defeat, Dick weeps gut-wrenching, small boy sobs.

Finally Dick's old real estate company agrees to take him back, but with the reservation that he work only on commission. Then, in a few months, company word comes through that Dick is not to use their stationery anymore. In short, they dismiss him in easy stages.

Dick has no interests to lead him to another kind of work, nor the ability to figure out how and where commercial real estate sites are opening up. While other men are making property deals out along the new Route 128, turning the highway into industrial gold, as their forebears once harnessed the rivers of New England, Dick turns an upstairs bedroom into an office and spends his days poring over his accumulation of family assets. We all pretend he still has a job.

✳

Summer 1958, and the Vineyard appears to be the same. The children have their daily life of swimming, sailing, biking, and tennis. The Irish girls say, "Sure, 'tis just like Ireland." But it isn't the same, and I'm a fool to lull myself into thinking it is.

A friend and I decide to take the weekend off and go up to the Berkshire Music Festival. Dick says he'll take charge of the children. Connie, an old friend, volunteers to run the children's games for me at the Saturday night dance and to watch out for Temple. Temple knows Connie well and has run in and out of her house as long as she can remember. All appear to be accounted for.

When I return home from the weekend, I learn that Dick ordered Temple to stay home from the Saturday night dance. Why, I don't know; everyone in the community always goes. Temple loves the dances, is well-behaved, and remembers with triumph the time when musical chairs got down to the last two contestants and she was one of them. She and the other contestant were blindfolded and had to grope for the one last chair, always moved, of course, from its original spot. Everyone cheered and threw out hints when one of them came near the chair.

"And I almost won!"

Remembering the excitement of it, hoping, perhaps, to win this time, knowing that I'd given her permission to go, Temple had dressed herself in her best, complete to scratchy petticoat, and walked three houses up the road to the casino where the dance was always held.

What happened next I learn from Connie. "All of a sudden, this frightened little face looks in the casino window at me. It's Temple. 'Help,' she cries, rapping on the glass. 'He's coming to take me home.' Next, Dick appeared, and he was livid. I put myself in front of Temple and said to him, 'Look Dick, she's afraid of you.' He said something like 'Nonsense, she's over dramatizing.' At that, Temple bolted and ran into Faffie's house."

I pick up the rest of the story from Faffie.

"I don't recall where in my house I found Temple, only that she was terrified. I don't remember what I said to her, but it worked and she calmed down enough to go home. I must have tried to put my arms around her because I remember she didn't want me to touch her."

What is hard to bear about this incident is that Temple, at this stage in her life, is happily gregarious and wants to please. Sadly, oddly, as she grows in confidence and poise, Dick is more and more obsessed to prove her uncontrollable, bearing down hard on her and frightening her. If I'm there, I can usually talk him out of it. If I'm not, temper, tears, and flight are all Temple has for a defense. Then Dick says, "See? She's out of control. What more proof do you want?"

It's Catch 22.

Grateful to Dedham Country Day School for their wisdom in guiding Temple, I volunteer to run the school fair. The fair's a combination neighborhood event and school money raiser. I talk various parents into manning the game booths and buy prizes for the game from a carny shop somewhere in the bowels of Boston. I hire a carnival Fire Engine, a pony and a small Ferris Wheel. That's it. That's all? Shouldn't we have something more, something new and exciting? I talk it over with another mother.

"How about putting on a show during the lunch break?" I ask her. "We could charge admission and make some extra money."

"Something geared to the younger children? Maybe a story like

Ferdinand? Why not?"

"*Ferdinand!* Perfect! We'll dress up the fathers and make them play matadors."

"And sing a funny song to *Carmen.*"

"What a hoot! The kids'll love seeing Dad make a fool of himself!"

By now, the Wampatuck Gang has picked up on our giggling excitement and is hopping all around us.

"We want to be in it too! Can we make scenery? Real scenery?"

"Yes, yes, we have to figure it out first!"

"I'll call George MacLeany." George is a Boston stage electrician. "I'll see if he'll lend us stage lights."

I call George and he promises to bring stage lights the day before the fair and hang them for us.

"We can't pay you," I warn him.

"That's OK. I'll charge it to the circus."

"Real lights!" the children squeal. "Real lights from the circus?"

We make up a script from *Ferdinand* and cast it. For rehearsals and scenery building, the school allows us full use of the auditorium every day after 3:00 p.m. The day before the fair, George arrives with lights and, most amazing of all, a flash pot.

"I thought you might like to play around with this?" A flash pot is a little gunpowder explosive connected to wires and lit by a ground spot. George demonstrates. "You throw the switch here, the gun powder goes off and the ground spot lights up the smoke. What color smoke do you want?" He holds out colored light gels to the children. "Pick a color, any color." The children choose green. George throws the switch and the flash pot goes off with a green puff. The children pound each other and shriek. We swear them to secrecy, knowing full well they can't wait to run outside and tell the whole neighborhood.

The show's a great success. The fathers cavort around in matador capes singing: "Toreador-a, don't spit on the floor-a. Use the cuspidor-a." Someone's child plays Ferdinand and sits under the cork tree smelling flowers and refusing the bull ring. Somebody's mother plays his mother the cow, and sings, "I Didn't Raise My Boy To Be a Soldier." Then, a kindergartner in a black and yellow union suit buzzes on stage and stings Ferdy. POW! The green flash pot goes off, and Ferdy leaps into the bullring. I forget the rest. Ask Temple. I bet she can still sing the songs.

As usual Dick is annoyed.

"Why do you have to put on a play? Nobody else puts on a play at the school fair!" I keep my mouth shut and churn. Taking my silence for contrition, Dick continues. "Why do you have all these ideas? I don't have them. You shouldn't have them." Then, in the following breath, "Everybody wants you. The children want you, Dedham Country Day School wants you, Sunday School wants you, and I want you."

I feel a stab of distress for him. He's in bad shape these days, but his temper's grown much more ominous, leaving me swinging back and forth between genuine sympathy and genuine fright. The siblings, aware of it, are suffering from the constant undercurrent of anxiety.

Except for Temple, who at this moment is bicycling furiously around Wampatuck Circle, oblivious to everything but the bicycle kite she's constructed. She's hitched it onto the back of her bike but, as yet, can't get up enough speed to make it lift out of the dust behind her.

"Rockabye *Ferdy* under a tre-e-e-e," she sings, this time pedaling with all her might, faster and faster round Wampatuck Circle. "When you sit down, don't sit on a bee!" The kite lifts and soars.

I leave the house, start the car, and head for Route 1, to Cambridge and the Poets Theatre. Out on Route 1, I turn onto an abandoned dirt road, stop, pull off my suburban sweater and put on my black beatnik sweater, laughing at myself, knowing how dumb it is, still hoping against hope that the sweater will win me the Poets Theatre password. I top it off with my mother's haughty expression, the nearest I can come to a "Nouvelle Vague" movie queen's pout. But like the black satin evening gown, it doesn't go with my face.

"Today," I tell myself, as I pull out of the dirt road and back onto Route 1, "I'll find out about auditions and, if I get a part, I'll make it count for a year's excitement," knowing all the while that any role I play will be contaminated with guilt. I reach Cambridge, turn into a parking lot, and guilt evaporates. I love everything about the Poets Theatre including the rain or shine stage exits onto the fire escape and down Palmer Street to Morris Pancoast's antique shop.

The Poets Theatre is preparing for a production of T. S. Eliot's verse play, *The Family Reunion*. It's the tale of a disastrously unhappy family, the plot based on the *Oresteia*. In the Aeschylus play, Orestes, after a series of blood baths, is pursued by the Furies until he turns and faces them. Only on facing them does Athena in her mercy change the Furies into the Eumenides, the Blessed Ones. Guilt, expiation and transformation. I'd read the play as a freshman, in F. 0. Mattheissen's course on Greek drama, which my dean had urged me to take.

"You can always take Doc Davison's music course," she'd advised me. "But we don't know how long we'll have Professor Mattheissen with us."

She was right. I was deeply moved by the *Oresteia,* and by Mattheissen himself, a small bald man who the next year threw himself out of a top story window in the Manger Hotel.

I climb the stairs to the tiny theatre space and learn that the

Eliot auditions have been scheduled for the following week. I buy a copy of *The Family Reunion* at the Coop, take it home to read and think about Eliot's own life, how he couldn't cope with his wife's glandular imbalance and, in desperation, banished her to an institution. Eliot, so the gossip goes, thought he'd killed his wife's soul, and all these years has been lugging that guilt around inside himself like a dead fetus that can never come to term. When I read the play, I see how deftly he's used his pain, woven it into the ancient *Oresteia* with the frayed threads of his unhappy WASP upbringing.

A few nights later, in the pouring rain, I go to hear Eliot in person at Sanders Theatre. I sit in the front row and listen to his urbane, self-deprecating observations on the staging problems of *The Family Reunion,* his guilty fetus reduced to an everyday theatrical task.

"The play doesn't work theatrically," he says, and, perhaps, it doesn't. Even with its exquisite poetry, the story is too internal for drama. "There was no way to stage the appearance of the Eumenides without their looking silly."

Trying to expiate pain with a verse play; perhaps that's what is silly. Perhaps only a small recognizable pain should be cut and faceted for today's theatre, a little gem set high in its prongs to catch the spotlight. Eliot's pain is too appalling to be ornamental.

The lecture winds down. I notice that Eliot has kept on his rubbers and wonder if they've made his feet hot.

The next week I return and audition for the role of Agatha, though I know I'm too young for it. The lines vibrate in me, but their inference escapes, lodging somewhere among the things I'm still choosing not to understand. Yet in the act of auditioning, they set up an echo. If I do get the part, will I ever be able to return to the little girl with the grade B movie dream?

Does that mean divorce? I allow the reality of the word to sink in deeper than I've ever before allowed it. If I leave my marriage, will I destroy Dick's soul, as Eliot thought he had destroyed his wife's soul? What about my four children?

> *It is the conversations not overheard*
> *Not intended to be heard, with the sidewise looks*
> *That bring death into the heart of a child.**

I am cast as Agatha, and Eliot's words take hold. Frightened and immature, unaware that Temple will succeed beyond my wildest dreams, I only know that Eliot is singing and I must follow his song.

> *The knot shall be unknotted*
> *And the crooked made straight**

Summer's over, and it's not over. The weeds hang limp and the heavy September air is working up to a storm. We're back from the Vineyard and, as usual, school has started up in a heat wave. Temple, now thirteen, has graduated from Dedham Country Day School and entered a much bigger, all-girl school. Her Viennese doctor is on the school board and thinks she can manage it, but, when I ask Temple how it's going, she tells me what she's had for lunch. A tip-off that she's not too happy.

Dick, adrift and angry, has decided to write a book to prove that God doesn't exist and all religion is meaningless. Is it to show me up for teaching Sunday School or because he's angry at my Episcopalian mother, her remarks about his family's loyalty to the Congregational Church?

"If you want us to go to the Congregational Church, I'd be happy to go there," I reply, "But since you don't want to go to *any* church, I'm going to go to the Episcopal Church."

Dick chews his cheek. I've implied that I don't take his religious project seriously, and he feels powerless. Without a job, family

---

* T.S. Eliot. *The Family Reunion*, 1939.

money is all that Dick has now for a sense of power. Family money makes him feel that whatever utility goes wrong in our house, he can always call some company manager and get quick redress. In truth, he can, that's the power of old money. At the same time, with no job, he's lost touch with the ordinary, power that comes from earning a daily living. As a result, he sees his family as draining him of power, and it makes him angry. In a sense, we are draining him. He has to pay for us.

I say nothing. I've learned to keep still in moments like this, lest the least retort or gesture trigger the violence that's roiling in Dick just under the surface. Instinctively, the siblings, too, keep very still; they've learned to take refuge in each other. But it has never occurred to me to warn Temple.

The electrician arrives to repair the refrigerator. After opening up its innards, he shakes his head, puts it back together again, and says we need new parts. Dick overhears, comes pounding down the stairs, bellows at the electrician that he doesn't know what he's doing, that he's going to report him and he won't pay the service charge. The electrician, now equally worked up, tells me to tell Dick that neither he, nor anyone else from his company, will ever service the house again. In the interests of having a working refrigerator, I assure the electrician there will be no unfavorable report, soothe his wounded pride, and pay the service charge.

The storm does not materialize. Instead a late, hot sun beats in the dining room window. We sit down to dinner. I read a story aloud, but nobody listens, and the children get into a grabbing contest over a squeeze bottle of catsup. Temple squeezes too hard and catsup squirts across the table. Dick leaps up with an oath.

"You little bitch!"

Temple runs from the table into the living room, Dick catches her, throws her down into an armchair, and grabs her by the neck. She gives his tie a hard yank. The knot cuts into his throat. He yells. She's out the door and down the road, Dick after her shouting, "Goddamn you! I'm going to kill you!"

The siblings and I quake on the front steps. "Is Daddy really going to kill her?"

"Oh God, I hope not." Is that all I can say? Why am I standing on the front porch wringing my hands?

Temple scrambles over the stone wall and disappears into the woods. Dick comes back up the road, his mouth tight. I can't tell if it's from rage at Temple or shame that he's come so close to brutality. I pretend nothing has happened and leave him to eat his dessert alone.

After a while Temple comes back and goes up to her room. "I hid in the poison ivy," she tells me. "I knew Daddy wouldn't want to get poison ivy."

Is that how it played out? I can't remember. The black hole has suddenly opened up again and swallowed the moment.

Later, Temple tells me that I did act, that I came screaming down the road, battered Dick's chest with my fists, dragged him off her.

"He was going to smash me against the wall."

Why have I no recollection of it?

Temple claims to have no emotions. That's why, she says, she can remember it all with perfect clarity.

But she was terrified!

In that moment I struck. I, who've always feared that Dick would strike me. And in committing the physical act I've split apart all semblance of domestic partnership, so wide apart it can never be put together again. From now on, Dick will open fire on me with the full force of his festering humiliation.

Is that what I can't bring myself to remember?

*

To all appearances, the September episode is behind us, and life is back to its old routine. Dick keeps office hours in the upstairs bedroom. When he isn't working on his God book, he copies down stock figures, adding them up over and over. Stocks are his comfort; they're what his father taught him, what the Grandin men discuss endlessly and are good at.

Then an angry thought catches him. Angry thoughts catch him often these days. He stops, writes his thought down longhand in a notebook. Next, he types out a letter to me and leaves it on my side of the bed. Later, when I try to defend myself, he takes my defense, shuffles it into another context, and round and round the old circle we go. I hear myself repeating the same words, "Yes, that's what I said, but that's not what I meant."

To get us out of it, I suggest to Dick that if he's undertaking a serious book on the value or lack of value in religious thought, why not study philosophy and comparative religion at the Harvard Divinity School? He says he doesn't need any divinity school; he can find all the facts he needs in books. Later, I see what he's underlined in red pen in our encyclopedia: extraneous bits backing up his convictions but not what's cogent to the paragraph. Yes, that's what the encyclopedia says, but that's not what it means. Dick says he knows what it means: religion is a crock dreamed up by people who want to feel better about themselves.

I decide to return to the marriage counselor psychiatrist whom Dr. Meyer had recommended so many years earlier, and, this time, I persuade Dick to see him too. Like Dr. Caruthers, the counselor is stout and avuncular. I see him now, tipping back in his old desk chair with its roller wheels and worn leather arms, his feet dangling off the floor, his plump fingers fitting another cigarette into his black filter holder. This wise, kindly man who lets me weep out my alarm without urging me into insights or looking at his watch, who tells me it was a toss-up when he was young whether to be a psychiatrist or an actor, sensing perhaps that the two roles aren't far apart. He holds in my heart much the same place as my singing teacher, also stout, also short, an old world voice teacher in whose worn baritone I always hear the great arias. Sensing my love of lyric, my need to sing to stay alive, he assigns me more French art songs and gives me half my singing lessons for free. The two men become my infrastructure.

I tell the psychiatrist I fear Dick's escalating rages and long to be divorced.

"It's getting to be like *Gaslight*. Dick unnerves me so. I no longer know if I'm right or wrong. I'm afraid not just for Temple but for all my children, and I keep thinking, if I lose it, who'll protect them? Maybe the answer is to stay home all day. But when I'm out in the world, people seem to find me acceptable, even worthwhile. If I lose that, I'll lose all sense of my own existence. Dick says it doesn't matter what I do; I'm hopelessly neurotic. Am I?"

"No, but you will be if you stay home all day. Thus far, you've been able to be a buffer between Dick and Temple. But remember, if you get divorced, Dick will have visiting rights with the children and at those times you won't be there to protect them."

"I can't believe Dick would actually hurt them. When all is said and done, he loves his children, and he loves me."

"No, he doesn't love you. He's obsessed with you. That's something quite different." The psychiatrist gives me a look. "Never underestimate his desire to punish you."

I don't know how to answer, even how to think. I want to take a running leap down the black hole.

"Then it's true; it really is *Gaslight*? For God sake, explain him to me!" The psychiatrist shakes his head.

"I can't, really, I don't understand him myself. I don't even understand his humor. He tells me things, he laughs at them, but I don't get what he's laughing at. I do know when he's angry; that's when he puts off paying the bill."

I go home. I find Dick waiting for me, ready with his anger over my extravagance.

"When I married you, you didn't waste money."

"Dick, when we married there were just two of us. Now we have four children and the two Irish girls. That's eight people."

"It's not the house money. It's that damn shrink. We have to cut down. We don't need him."

"We do need him. He's on the board of Temple's new school. He knows the headmaster. It's only because of him that Temple's been accepted there."

"I'm not talking about Temple, I'm talking about you! You don't need a shrink. You're an egotist. That's your trouble!"

I grope for an answer; fright garbles my tongue.

"Just say it in words of one syllable!"

"I'm trying to."

"No, you're not. You're showing off your vocabulary!"

I try to grab the thread of my thought, but my throat tightens and the words are gone. My throat hurts all the time now, so whatever I say emerges stilted and over elaborate. OK, so I'm an egotist. An egotist with a sore throat.

I talk to Dick's brother's wife.

"Dick is alone all day now. Every day he's in that upstairs bedroom, checking stock figures and poring over his religious documents. He needs a job, any job. Can't his brother help him find work?"

No help is forthcoming.

Winter 1960. In spite of my sore throat, I accept a small role in a Poets Theatre production, an English translation of a Polish play brought from behind the Iron Curtain. The play's action takes place in a Polish prison and revolves around the emotional lockhold between guard and prisoner, each so justifying the role of the other that the two ultimately change places. The director directs it as a farce. I play the guard's unhappy wife.

During rehearsals, a man named Hermann Field comes up the theatre stairs to watch us. When we take a break he tells us, though the play's premise may seem absurd to us, it's actually close to the truth. And the madness of farce is the only way to play it.

Farce. Madness. Infant schizophrenia. Temple. My mind wanders off for a bit to wrestle with that perilous sequence. Forcing my attention back to what Field is saying, I hear him tell us that he's just returned from behind the Iron Curtain where he went in search of his brother, Noel Field.* Because he was Noel's brother, he was arrested by the Communists, and from then on, Hermann Field says, the days of his own life played out exactly like our play. Convinced that he must have vital U.S. State Department spy information, the Russians kept him closely jailed, taking him out every day for long interrogations until— what with the cold, the lack of food, and the interrogation process—he fell ill with a high fever. When the Russians brought in a doctor to dose him with penicillin, Field realized that they didn't want him to die and take spy information with him to the grave. That much was good to know, Field acknowledged, but the problem still remained: he had nothing to confess.

---

* In preparing the frame-up of Hungary's communist leaders, Stalin needed the image of American anti-Soviet intrigue as the supposed trigger for massive subversion within his ranks. The focus fell on Noel Field. © 1999, 2000 Hermann & Kate Field.

"It began to be madness. My cellmate and I wrote a novel together on toilet paper to keep from going crazy."

"Why didn't you make up a confession?" we ask.

"I finally decided to do just that," Field replies. "I worked out a confession that would tally with the gist of what the Russian seemed to be after. But when I told the guards I was ready to confess, the guards said that it was Friday afternoon. They were leaving for the weekend; I could confess on Monday. Over the weekend, Stalin died, and everyone in the prison was released, including me."

Who exactly are Hermann and Noel Field, and do I really want to know? What with the Cold War and the recent McCarthy hearings, if Dick hears Field's story, he'll say the Poets Theatre is Communist. Resonating deeply at this moment is the similarity between the play, Hermann Field's story, and the way Dick grills me. Then when the weekend comes, how Dick drops his grilling and goes back to being his old friendly self. Once again, I believe in his friendliness, believe he understands what I am trying to do for Temple, even sympathizes with it—then, whop! It's Monday and he's after me again, using my own words against me, taking them out of context, twisting them around to say something else.

Farce or madness? Either way it's desperately awry. I know that I'm the lone community rebel in a Republican enclave. I know that the morning after Kennedy's election, my car has been plastered with Nixon stickers because I voted for Kennedy. I accept all that. But I also see that the community accepts Temple and accepts me. The Grandin family accepts me; Dick's sister keeps defending me.

Where are Dick's rages coming from? Why do they erupt suddenly for no reason then for no reason disappear just as suddenly?

Dick has limited interests and limited insight. He lives and intends to live by a rigid social pattern he learned in his young days. He has money and financial ability but somehow, he missed out on the formal business education that would have led him to a suitable investment position. His job as a real estate agent never has been a calling; rather, it's something he fell into at a time when everybody in the postwar boom was having babies and needed a bigger house.

He's accepted my decision not to institutionalize Temple; and accepted Temple. He's even grown fond of her. And Temple has thrived in his lifestyle. Better yet, she's been accepted into it unconditionally. The Leave-it-to-Beaver world has been Temple's salvation.

Nevertheless, there will always be a catch to both of us. Temple and I share that pushy little renegade gene. We'll always chafe at a conservative leash and it has nothing to do with autism. We aren't either of us cut out to be shy violets. Temple may have been fearful when she was little and speechless, and her fears may erupt again when she reaches adolescence, but right now she's the first in the family to introduce herself to new neighbors. Self-abnegation isn't her style.

Nor is it mine. However much Dick frightens me with his grilling—and he genuinely frightens me—I can never quite hold back the risible hoyden gene that wells up in uncanny opposition to his conservative nature. Oblivious to his genuine distress at having the Grandin name bandied about in cheap gossip columns, I've sung in a bookie joint and taken it as a joke.

Had Dick married a more conservative woman, siring only "normal" children—whomever they may be—he probably would have slid home safe. But he isn't attracted to quiet homebodies; the hoyden gene delights him even when it throws him off balance. What he can't see is that the very qualities he loves and hates are those that have enabled me to step outside the usual ethos of the Leave-it-to-Beaver world and make my own decisions about Temple. Temple's Viennese doctor may be right. Oil and water don't mix.

I have no problem playing the part in the Polish play of the guard's defeated wife. I know the role by heart.

During the day when the children are in school, I sing to comfort myself. Dick, in his upstairs room, complains of the noise and has the living room soundproofed. Why now? I've sung for years and he hasn't minded it. My sore throat is getting worse. Why don't I just stop? No, I don't want to. I can't bear to.

A few weeks later, the taste of blood fills my mouth. I go to an ear, nose, and throat doctor, a friend and neighbor whose children play with my children. He seats me in his examining chair, wraps a piece of gauze around his hand, takes hold of my tongue and pulls it out. I gag. Gentle, but firm, he pulls it out further. I gag again.

"I need to look at your vocal chords."

My vocal chords? The root of the sound of the complicated words? The doctor pulls again.

"Agggghhhhhhhh." I choke and drool. A memory of Temple at three years old scums to the surface of my mind. She stands by my desk, unable to speak. She grabs at me, holds out her ball, tries to say the word "ball," but it comes out "bahhh." Like a protesting sheep. She knows the word, but she can't get it out—"bahh, bahh—" over and over. Or is it me gagging?

The doctor peers down my throat, all the way to my "say-it-in-words-of-one-syllable" vocal chords. "Ahh-ahh"—that's all I can say. Finally the doctor lets go.

"You've broken the blood vessels in your vocal chords."

"Is that why I taste blood?"

"Yes." He pauses. "I'm afraid you won't ever sing again." Silent, I swallow blood. My tongue throbs from the wrench of his pull.

"You mustn't speak out loud for six weeks."

I can't speak anyway. The doctor goes on.

"You'll have to whisper. The point is to try to retain your speaking voice. You don't want to end up talking like Louis Armstrong. He has broken vocal chords from blowing a trumpet, that's what makes his voice gravelly."

"I've agreed to direct a play next summer," I whisper.

"You better not."

I struggle with this. I swallow to ease my tongue into feeling like my own again. The doctor waits. He's patient, he's aware. His violation of my tongue is purely medical. Finally I whisper, "It's my sanity or my chords."

"OK, I understand. Summer's a long way off. Please, for your own good, whisper for at least six weeks. And, then, maybe. But, remember, you can't stand in the back of the hall and yell at the actors. You'll have to figure out another way."

He unfastens the bib from round my neck and gives me a towel to wipe the drool from my chin.

I go home, I tell Dick. He's kindness itself. And why not? His mission is accomplished: no more acting; no more singing; no more words.

The next evening Dick listens attentively to a group from the theatre we've invited for dinner. We sit at the table, and he impresses them with his sincerity. For the moment he believes in it, believes sincerely he's a man who wants to know, wants to understand.

A young black actor complains about the theatre director. The next production is now in rehearsal, and the director has staged a fight scene at a dining table.

"What a dumb way to stage a scene full of anger," the actor says. "How can I express anger when I'm eating? I can choke on the food—like this—I can chew on it like this—" He does a brilliant improv. "What else can I do to express anger when I have to swallow food?"

I'm angry, but I have no trouble swallowing. I can sit here and swallow all this guff.

An older woman, a patroness of the theatre, secure in her high ideals and her sophistication, takes me aside after dinner to have an insightful talk.

"Your husband is a very wonderful man. He understands; he wants to understand. That's very important you know."

She sermons on, her words not a suggestion but a command. I can't talk, so I have plenty of time to look her over: her expensive dress, her amber beads, the blood red lipstick running into the lines on her upper lip. She is "au courant" with culture fodder. Art, theatre, poetry readings: she consumes them all. That doesn't mean she's all accepting. Oh, no. I'm clearly not on her acceptance list. She's seen me flirt with an actor and she disapproves.

There's no way to explain it to her, even if I could speak. My throat aches; I swallow blood. Yes, I know: Dick wants to understand, but, more important, he wants to control me and, for the time being, he's achieved it, so he can afford to be understanding. What does it cost him to impress this self-impressed woman whom he will never see again with his sincerely magnanimous desire to understand? To understand what? Me? Temple? His job loss? Does he feel safer now that I'm diminished? He can let down his guard, is that it? Loosen his stranglehold? And this woman believes him; her belief costs her nothing. Everybody feels fine. I listen, silent and shamed. Somewhere in this smirking round of sincerity, I feel Dick's lash. I've been brought low. We're even now, better than even. He's top dog.

The next day I close the piano lid, put away the sheet music, buy a whistle to get the children to pay attention to my whisper, and pray that Temple will keep out of the range of Dick's fire.

It will be three years before I can speak normally and seven years before I can act or sing. A minor miracle that it happens at all.

In the meantime, speech taken from me, as once, long ago, it was taken from Temple, I return to reading omnivorously. Whether to understand what's happening or to retreat into the old habit of denial, I'm not yet sure.

I take down the Bible my grandmother gave me when I was a girl—my grandmother who listened to my ramblings, took my thoughts seriously, whom I now miss more than I can bear to think about—open the crumbling leather cover and look at the inscription: "Anna Eustacia Purves."

It's been years since I've seen my full name. I'd almost forgotten the "Anna" part. Anna was her name.

"September 12th 1935."

She must have given it to me on my ninth birthday. Nine. That's younger than Temple. Her handwriting is angular and I realize how, under stress, my own handwriting has turned as angular as hers. I leaf through the frail tissue pages with their worn gilt borders.

Genesis: "And the Lord God formed man of the dust of the ground, And breathed into his nostrils the breath of life; and man became a living soul."

Eve seems to have been an afterthought, not shaped from the dust by God's potter hand, nor turned on His wheel, nor even given a name. The Lord God fashioned her from a rib stolen from Adam during a nap, dolled her up and gave her back to Adam to keep him company. Only after both are barred from

Eden does Adam, not the Lord God, name her "Eve."

"Eve, the troublemaker!" I can just hear Adam shouting it at her. "Eve, who can't leave well enough alone! Who has to know. Who has to eat it!"

Tears, long held back, prick my nose with their salt.

No—wait—I refuse to weep. I did not originate sin. Imperfect, yes, but doing the best I can and not responsible for Adam's name calling. If I can't speak, can't sing, can't act, I'll search out sin on my own: search through the vast army of unidentified maimed, find sin where it's hiding and touch the wounded viscera for myself.

Me, the extravert and introvert. The show-off and the perpetual student.

The show-off has long since begun the search. For years I've entertained damaged GI's in the wards of the local Vet Hospitals, singing to men who've lost their faces and are waiting for the skin grafts they pray will make them look human again. I've sung in the locked wards to the vets who've lost their minds. They're still handsome, those young catatonics whose faces have turned to stone, whose bodies are frozen in any old posture like a game of "Statues."

"If I Knew You Were Coming I'd Have Baked a Cake." I've sung that song and here and there I've seen a foot tap. Everything else is rigid; just one foot keeping time to the music, tapping on a cell wall, alive inside that cell, tapping out messages no one knows how to answer.

Now I, too, am reduced to tapping. I'll tap on a typewriter. Yes, but where do I start, and what do I tap?

Sometimes a stroke of luck comes your way—not as my father thought through intense theoretical concentration, but through a friend. In this case, Temple's friend, Lyman.

The phone rings. It's Lyman's mother.

"The Junior League of Boston is undertaking two television documentaries for WGBH: the first on retarded children; the second on troubled children. Would you consider rejoining the League and working on them?"

Chapter 6

And Start All Over Again

September 1960. I take the cue from Lyman's mother, rejoin the Junior League and begin the long process of researching the mapless face of retardation. Every morning right after the children leave for school, I set forth for "terra incognita."

First assignment: medical school instruction on retardation at the Massachusetts General Hospital. The doctor who's guiding me admits that this one class is all the instruction the medical students will get on the subject. Future doctors are not much interested in studying retardation.

Next assignment: a clinic where the social problems of the retarded are addressed. A mother brings in her son, a gentle, blonde teenager with no visible sign of retardation. He's been promoted through high school, she says, without ever being taught to read and write.

"He could have learned if the school had been willing to help him. I told them he was slow, but the school wouldn't listen and now it's too late. My son's a good boy, but he can't speak up for himself. He wants a job pumping gas but no one will hire him because he can't write out a slip for the gas."

The boy sits beside her, handsome, a little dim, but not too dim to hope.

Field work: Monson State Hospital. Monson, I'm told, harbors every variety of human imperfection: goblins, pinheads, cretins. The dictionary politely defines "cretin" as coming from the French word "cretin" meaning Christian, hence a human being. But the French dictionary avoids any such euphemism, bluntly translating "cretin" as "idiot or dunce."

Armed with a road map and a notebook, I drive to the outskirts of a small New England town, park and find my way into a quadrangle of brick buildings enclosing the village green of Monson State Hospital.

As I walk up the path to the main building I see a group of children raking leaves. Coming closer I realize they're "mongoloids," so called because of the Asian cast to their faces. The next generation will call them "Down Syndrome" children, will raise them at home as part of the family, and star them in Special Olympics. But this is 1960. We banish them to remote institutions like Monson, and put them to work raking leaves, washing clothes, cooking, ironing, and caring for the more retarded.

In the reception hall I meet the head nurse who takes me on a tour, first to a "closed workshop," by definition a workshop no outsider sees. Seated at a long table is a group of the more retarded stuffing mailers into envelopes and sealing them. From now on, when I throw out advertising mail, I will wonder who stuffed and sealed those envelopes.

In another workshop rows of the severely retarded are pulling apart sterilized horsehair to be stuffed into new mattress covers. The old, urine-soaked horsehair tangles and mats in the sterilizer, and has to be pulled apart by machine. The head nurse, whose dedication springs from her devotion to a retarded brother, has discovered that her patients like to pull it apart by hand. She's set up this room for them, told them this is to be their job.

"In life everybody has a job. Your job is to pull apart the horsehair."

"Yes! We want a job, we want to be like everybody."

"Then you must learn to use the toilet and dress yourself and make your bed. That's what everybody does."

Rocking and giggling, they agree. "Yes, that's what we want."

"Then, after you dress, you have breakfast, and then you walk to work in another building. Everybody goes to work in another place. That's what 'going to work' is."

"Oh. That's going to work?"

"Yes, and you'll earn money. Everybody earns money."

"Money?"

"See? This is money." She shows them nickels and dimes. "You can buy candy." Thus with coaxing, penny change, and long patient hours the nurse has drawn her charges out of their idiot lethargy and given them the rudiments of human purpose.

"These people aren't capable of much," she tells me, "they're very retarded. But you can't just leave them to rot. When I first came here they were sitting on benches around the room, naked. 'Why aren't they dressed,' I asked? The staff said 'It's no use to dress them, they tear their clothes off.' So I said, 'If you're going to treat them that way, why don't you put a drain in the middle of the floor and shut the door on them?' You wouldn't treat a dog that way.'"

Then she explains, a little embarrassed, "You see, because they were naked, they had nothing to do except masturbate. Well, I thought, if they like to masturbate, I'll use that. I figured the horsehair from the mattresses would feel to them like pubic hair. And I thought, they'll like the feeling of pulling it apart. We won't turn the pulling job over to a machine, I'll make it into a job for them. And pretty soon, because they like their job, they won't tear their clothes off. And it worked, I taught them to dress, to use the toilet, to make their beds, to walk to work, and to do their job, their horsehair job, right here in this room. And over time I've seen their faces change. People think the retarded don't feel anything, but that's not true. As soon as they feel they matter, they lose their vacant expression and begin to look human."

I ask her if she'd be willing to tell her story for the WGBH documentary and reluctantly she agrees to it.

We walk down one more endless hall. Bang! goes a linen closet door and out storms a stout middle-aged woman with a shaved patch in her ragged Dutch cut and a freshly healed scar: tokens of an epileptic seizure.

"Well, she can go to hell and kiss my arse!" She sees the head nurse. "Honest to Gawd, Miss Essie, I never lied! So help me! Cross my heart and kiss the virgin I didn't take 'em!"

"Shh, shh, Abby. Hey, what's got into you today?"

"Honest to Gaaawwd," howls Abby. "I get so miserable, I just took a little piece. Nobody loves me—nobody writes me—I get so lonesome—don't get no letter—don't get no candy." The howl rises to a wail. "She gets packages every weeeeek!"

"You could of bought candy. You got last week's wages."

"I don't want wages—I don't deserve 'em—I was naughty and Dr. MacIver bawled me out for throwing the thermometer in the toilet. Honest to Gawd, Miss Essie—I didn't mean to break it, only Donna jostled me—Oooh I hate her! She's a mean bitch and she can kiss my—"

"Abby—you didn't learn those words from me."

"Aw Miss Essie, you're a kidder—everbody knows those words—everbody knows 'em from the time they're kids. Gawd I love you, Miss Essie—I'm gonna give you a kiss and I won't take no more chocolate 'cause I'm gonna be a good girl for you and get my badge."

The institution doctor comes down the hall. "Hi there, Abby, how's your boyfriend?"

"Aw Dr. MacIver, I got no boyfriend. Who'd want a funny lookin' girl like me?" She shows me her scar. "See? I got this big place here where I bang my head—come over here—you can't see me from over there!"

"Roy'd want you."

"Aw Dr. MacIver, you're kiddin'—how'd you know about Roy?"

"I got eyes in the back of my head."

Later that month the WGBH crew brings sound equipment, lights and a camera into the horsehair room. The head nurse tries to tell her story, but the camera unnerves her. I sit under it.

"Don't look at the camera. Look at me, tell your story just to me, just like before."

"I'm worried I won't speak the right grammar, I'll make mistakes and sound stupid."

By this time all the excitement over the lights and camera has stirred up her patients, the horsehair pullers. They stop their work, begin to rock and call out—to me, to the director, the camera man, the sound man—"Hey nursie—" Everybody is "nursie." "Take my picture. You going to take my picture?"

The nurse struggles to pull herself together, to pull them together. This is her chance to show the world that her people are worth something, that her brother deserves to be called "human."

"You're not going to be babies," she cries out. "You're not going to rock. Stop it! Do you hear me? Everybody—you pull hair!"

But they can't. The camera, the lights, it's all too strange. Forgetting her careful lessons in purpose, the entire room begins rocking back and forth like a bunch of cuckoo clock pendulums.

The nurse leaps up on a bench. "Come on!" she hollers, her voice cracking. "Are you men or are you babies!" One man stops rocking and looks up at her.

"Baby?"

The footage is useless. We move the equipment to another ward. Again the occupants call out.

"Hey Miss, come here Miss, look at me. See my funny little chicken arm. Brawk! Brawk!" He shows off his arm withered to nothing by brain damage, folded into his chest like a bat's wing. "Brawk, brawk, brawk. Didja ever see anything like that before? Hey Miss, you gonna take my picture? Miss, look how good I can do with my other arm." He clutches at me with his good arm.

"Let go, Billy." The nurse takes his good arm. "She's got your picture. That's a boy, let go."

In the next ward are humans so damaged, they're trapped for life in a birth-bruised chrysalis. Powerless to unfold, they lick mush from a spoon and smell the endless smell of urine and Lysol.

That's the end of the picture taking.

The next day I come alone to thank everybody.

"If you're going to write about the retarded," says Dr. MacIver, "you shouldn't leave without looking at the creatures."

"There's worse?" He nods.

"I'll go with you. It can be a shock." Like many country Yankees, he has a lantern jaw and few words.

The ward is sunny and silent, save for the crooning of an ancient idiot woman who sits by the door cradling a baby with a monstrous head, rocking it.

The doctor walks me round the ward. A towheaded toddler smiles and stands up in his crib. I look at the stumps of his baby hands grasping the crib rail. The ends of his fingers from the middle knuckle are gone. There's nothing there but blobs of flesh, wet and soft.

"He's eaten the ends of his fingers. He has no sensation of pain."

In the next crib lies a tiny rigid child of six, perfect in every proportion, but no more than a foot and a half long. The bones in her back and arms and legs are fused. She has no joints. The nurse has dressed her in doll's clothes.

In the next crib is a child with the strangest arms and legs I've ever seen. They wave in the air, long and thin, boneless as Bugs Bunny.

Next to her is a dark-haired boy with a head the size of a Mickey Mouse balloon and a body no more than twenty-four inches. His eyes are beautiful, with black lashes showing up against the stretched cheek bones of his encephalitic head. The cheek bones have splayed his teeth out over his lower lip. All that's there are his eyes, those beautiful eyes.

"How old is he?"

"Fourteen."

"How long will he live?"

"Forty, maybe. With antibiotics."

"Why not let him go?"

"Life is strong, it doesn't lie down and die just 'cause you want it to." The doctor's long, lined farmer face looks resigned. Both to the fate of the boy and his own limited fate as a small town doctor in a forgotten New England mill town, left to care for the severely damaged. Then seeing that I can't accept his answer, he adds, "We keep him alive not for him, but for us. Hitler decided to do away with the retarded and look where that took us."

We walk down the stairs, he stops. "Before you go, I'd like you to meet my son." In a nearby recreational room a boy is operating a hand loom with the help of an attendant.

"Hi-yah Johnny, how's a professah?" The doctor gives his boy an affectionate cuff, Johnny grabs his father's hand and kisses it. "Johnny's learning to work the handloom."

"And he's learning to read, too," the attendant says. Johnny nods, gurgles, holds up his book, and reads out a jumble of words.

Another affectionate pat and Dr. MacIver and I walk out into the autumn sunshine, past the children raking leaves. The doctor greets each child by name and I'm grateful for his close-mouthed Yankee goodness.

"Be fruitful and multiply," God whispers in our ear, and leaves us to deal with the mess. Something we call Mother Nature. All those DNA strands laid out so intelligently, then Mother Nature picks up her hasty knitting. Stitches dropped all over the place, one sleeve longer than the other—why have I taken on this hideous assignment?

That night when I get home I take a glass of gin into the shower with me and stand in the hot steam drinking it, hoping the gin and shower will wash me clean of the sights, the sounds, the smell, the pain, the loneliness, the boredom, the repulsion, the horror—and my own shame. I'm ashamed that I don't care for these weird, achingly human creatures. But I'm the one who's sought them out, I've incorporated them into myself and now—gurgling, tugging, and strangely dignified—they won't leave.

However intelligent I think I am, however charitable and reverent of life, lodged deep in my mindless dreams is a clammy anxiety over these poor beings. Fearing the very sight of them may cause some horrid contamination, I, too, want them shipped off. Out of sight.

No movie achieves this anxiety better than the thirties movie of *Frankenstein*, with its dark "German expressionism" shadows. In the movie the faithful, dimwitted Fritz is instructed to steal a brain from the Goldstadt Medical College. Through the window he watches Doctor Waldman hold forth on two brains, one a perfect and upright specimen, the other, ugh—

"Note," says Dr. Waldman, pointing to the abhorrent brain, tracing its whorls with his pencil, "the scarcity of convolutions on the frontal lobe, the distinct degeneration of the middle frontal lobe. These check amazingly with the history of the dead man before us whose life was one of brutality, violence and murder."

Dr. Waldman departs, the class files out, the laboratory lights turn ominously low.

Fritz enters by stealth, grabs up the jar marked "normal" only to drop it. Oh my, what to do? The perfect and upright brain lies shattered in a pool of formaldehyde. Fearful lest he displease Dr. Frankenstein, desperate for anything brain-like, though clearly he's been warned, he seizes the jar marked "dysfunctio cerebri," (also marked "abnormal brain" in case we can't read Latin) and the rest is movie history.

The movie make-up and monster costume give Boris Karloff the look of a huge and powerful hydrocephalic. A look Karloff reinforces with voice, clumsiness, and the slow, vaguely threatening response of limited comprehension.

Is the monster—he's called "the monster"—friendly? Yes, but I don't want his friendship. Will that make him angry? What will happen then? Fits of physical rage are not unknown in institutions for the retarded and those deemed mad. Strong male attendants are employed to keep a hand on things. Monstrous strength can be triggered by a seizure, or a new excitement. Am

I the new excitement? All suitable human feelings vanish. I don't want him to grunt his story at me! I don't want to learn that he has the same hunger for friends that I have—the same need to hug and be hugged, that he's really gentle at heart, that all he wants is to be listened to—

No! Every cell in me wants to run. But then, every cell in me wants to look. The creature is my shame-choked haunting.

Finally the gin does its work.

✳

Spring, 1961. The WGBH documentary on retardation, titled *The Innocents*, an old-fashioned term for the retarded, is given a private pre-airing screening before its public release.

Since it covers shots of St. Colletta's, a convent school for retarded children endowed by the Kennedy family in memory of the oldest Kennedy son, Joe Kennedy Jr., Ted Kennedy, the youngest son, attends the screening. He is surprisingly shy and solemn, taking his family duties seriously.

The Innocents, wins an "Ohio State" award for subject matter and for "always being honest," i.e. a first-time full-face presention of the retarded. Hard to believe, but up until now not even Down Syndrome children have been photographed for newspapers or television.

The Junior League, frequently ridiculed as an organization of Lady Bountifuls, deserves credit for originating an amazing first and producing it with WGBH—a documentary calculated to force their own comfortable, privileged world to face the hidden world of the severely retarded. Today at the screening I note to some big-wig that Eleanor Roosevelt began her life-long commitment to altruism as a member of the Junior League.

I brood on the separating out that we practice in our Leave-it-to-Beaver world. Doctors separate out the body organs, studying the heart, liver, brain, and kidney as if each were an entity unto itself with no relation to the other organs or the being who houses them all. Along with the biological separating out, goes the medical practice of separating out medical disciplines, each research project traveling parallel to the other with no cross reference.

But the most difficult are the social separatings. C. P. Snow has just published his 1959 Rede Lecture on the social division between science and literature. Straddling the two disciplines himself, Snow has learned firsthand how neither chooses to honor the imaginative understanding of the other. Instead, he says, "the feelings of one pole become the antifeelings of the other."*

A week later *The Innocents* is aired publically and Dick denounces it. I don't know why, my name is nowhere in the credits. Someone tells me I'm a neighborhood joke: "Dick Grandin is criticizing his wife again."

Despite local derision, I set to work to research the next documentary on "disturbed children" as most of us are still calling children with autism. This documentary is to be titled *The Disquieted*, from a passage in the psalms:

Why art thou cast down, 0 my soul?
and why are thou disquieted within me?

The state of Massachusetts, often educationally in the forefront, finances public school day classes for "special" children. Though the classes are excellent, the children attending them are mostly retarded. Autism, if recognized at all, is considered a psychosocial problem.

A psychiatrist takes me to a well-known psychiatric hospital with a residential unit for autistic children. As long as I live I will never forget stepping off the elevator onto that floor of silent, isolated children, each obsessed with some meaningless, repetitive

---

* C.P. Snow, *The Two Cultures and the Scientific Revolution*, Cambridge University Press, NY, 1961.

preoccupation. The silence takes my breath away.

"Please don't write about autism," the psychiatrist says. "We don't know what it is, we don't know what to do about it. You will only hold out hope and there is none."

That's her sum total diagnosis? Rage stomps through me. Every imperfection I've witnessed among the retarded and brain damaged seems more bearable, more explainable, more humane than this quick dismissal. But I soon realize that it isn't a dismissal, it's a plea, an open admission of medical bewilderment. The psychiatrist is conscientious, she's achieved good results with some of her less desperate patients, children whom she calls affectionately "sand in the machinery."* But here her conscience stops.

I search the faces of these withdrawn children in their silent Bedlam, this huge private playpen where no child plays with another, and wonder is this another place where Temple might have been sent? I think of Temple's nanny, her play sessions with Temple, her insistence that Temple be kept continually involved. I think of Mrs. Reynold's speech classes and Mrs. Huckle's camp. It's the middle of the day, why aren't these children in some kind of school set-up? What therapy and/or education are they receiving? Public school classes for the retarded look better than this.

But there my conscience stops, too. Fearing the label of "refrigerator mother," I decide not to tell the doctor about Temple, and not to ask the questions I know I ought to be asking. It's a cowardly act on my part, and one I will regret, but a feverish anxiety has come over me. The hospital is so impressive, the doctor is so impressive, and what I'm looking at is so appalling.

Instead I promise the doctor to leave the subject of autism out of the documentary, and cover only the disturbed children she and the other psychiatrists consider suitable, i.e. state institution children and court children who've been adjudicated delinquent.

I arrange an interview with a State House official, explain my

---

* Probably undiagnosed Asperger.

project to him, and ask if I may visit the city's juvenile courts and detention centers.

"OK, I'll let you in," the official says, "but don't you dare come back to me with some pat little answer!"

I try to talk him into letting me into the high school system, one school in particular that I've heard bad stories about.

"No, I won't let you in there. They just keep the lid on the garbage pail. You'll go, you'll write your sanctimonious distress, it'll get in the paper and everybody will pay attention for a day. One day. Then it's all forgotten and we're back to the same old garbage pail. I don't know what to do about it, so I just keep the lid on too."

We settle for what he will let me see: a detention center in Jamaica Plain where juvenile offenders between eight and eighteen are being held before formal sentencing.

The Jamaica Plain Detention Center for Boys is brick. I show my pass at the entrance, someone escorts me up the metal stairway and unlocks the metal grill door that opens into the holding room: a cement walled room surrounded by metal grill cubicles where social workers can conduct interviews. It's prison all right, reeks of Lestoil and sweat, reverberates nonstop with the milling crowd of boys. Some of them look like full-grown men, some, booked under the police catch-all "stubborn child," look hardly the required eight years of age. "Stubborn child" is an old court term for a boy arrested between the ages of eight and twelve for charges that are not fully clear. He could be a battered child removed from home by a social worker in order to safeguard him. He could have destroyed property. He could be an habitual truant and a petty thief. Or he could be autistic.

An autistic boy destroying property? That's understandable. Autistic children are good at destruction. Running away from school? If a child doesn't have a clue what school is about, running away may be his only solution. But I wonder how well an eight-year-old autistic boy would understand what a "crime" is. Longing for friends, he could easily be inveigled into joining older boys in a larcenous act he doesn't fully comprehend. Arrest might have no meaning for him either. To an isolated autistic child, arrest might feel like a bit more of what he hungers for: attention.

Court arrest means a boy has had three prior "booked" arrests. "Booked" arrests are not made until he's had three street arrests. So the boys in this detention center have had a total of nine arrests and are now being held pending a court decision. The detention center, though an advance over past penal systems, is still a prison: part bullpen, part cafeteria, and part social worker office.

I enter the bullpen and no boy so much as glances at me. It's assumed I'm a court social worker and none of them wants to be interrogated further. Then a small child spots me, runs across the pen and winds his skinny arms around my waist.

"Please lady. Tell her to come and get me." His head smells of dirt and through his institution buzz cut, I can see ancient crusts of cradle cap. Gulping, sobbing he pours out a story I can't make head or tail of.

A cop hovers nearby. "He wants his mother."

"Please, lady, please." The boy won't let go.

"I'll do what I can."

"Don't try to be the social worker," the cop warns me.

"What's he in for?"

"Stubborn child."

In spite of the cop, I find a social worker in one of the cubicles and ask about his case. She doesn't seem to know, so I ask if I can visit his mother. She disappears into her cubicle and comes back with an address scribbled on a scrap of paper. "If you go, don't sit down, not unless you want to come home with bugs."

I climb a stoop in South Boston and ring the bell. A grey doughy woman opens the door. I explain why I've come. Her eyes shift about, but used to obeying cops and social workers, she lets me in. I stand, there are no chairs. She looks too old to be his mother. Perhaps his grandmother?

"What's the trouble?" I ask. She sighs, shifts her weight exuding the smell of unwashed fat. Cagey, subservient, she recites what she thinks I want to hear, as she's recited it before to the cops and the judge. When I question her, she changes her story, winding up with the old catch-all. "Stubborn child."

"I can't do nothing with him."

She calls out a name and a girl appears, perhaps in her late teens—pale and scrawny, her bleached hair piled elaborately on the top of her head. She tells me she's his sister and recites a different tale. Nothing adds up. I keep hearing the word "truant," as if they're both glad to be rid of him.

I say goodbye and leave, weary with their hang dog evasions, their dingy survival skills, the whole sly mess. I've caught a whiff of the despair the State House official feels over his bad high school. That edgy moment when sympathy turns to irritation because you don't have a solution.

Discouraged, I move on to the next approved state target: The Children's Division of a State Institution.

Valentine's Day is coming and a group of eight-year-olds are making valentines. Red construction paper, scissors, pencils, and paste are laid out on the long table along with thin white tissue paper. I sit down with them and together we watch the teacher show us how to fold and cut the tissue paper into valentine lace.

113

At the end of the table, apart from the others, sits a boy who, again, looks barely eight years old. In the chair beside him is an empty plastic Dazzle bottle, a popular detergent.

"I can't get him to join in with the other children," the attendant whispers. "He carries that plastic jug with him everywhere, he sleeps with it. Sometimes I kid him and call him Old Dazzle Bottle."

I try to catch the boy's eye, but he won't look. I move down the table and sit beside him.

"How about a valentine?" He stares down at the table and pushes his sheet of red construction paper in front of me.

"Draw me a hundred hearts," he says, his eyes never lifting. I draw them. "Are you sure there're a hundred?" He won't look, won't count, so I count.

"Yes, they're a hundred." He pulls the red paper back and in the first heart he letters carefully the word "me."

"Isn't there someone you'd like for your valentine?" He shakes his head and continues to print "me" in the center of each of the hundred hearts. Finished, he slips off of his chair. I don't want to let him go.

"Is there someone you'd like to send your valentine to?" Again he shakes his head. He has what he wants. He picks up his valentine to himself, picks up his Dazzle bottle and trailing it like a teddy bear, heads down the corridor on some private mission.

No response, no desire for one. And no eye contact. Even a puppy will catch your eye and bound over for attention. What about fear? A rustle in the dry leaves will send a squirrel up a tree. What's going on in the growing emptiness of Old Dazzle Bottle?*

My next stop is a state school where, if they're lucky, the eight-

---

* Recently I asked a trained psychologist cop if he thought Charles Manson was autistic. "No," he said. "Just anti-social. But I think Jeffrey Dahmer was."

year-olds, adjudicated delinquent in the Jamaica Plain Detention Center, are sent to be rehabilitated. A young psychiatrist, a skilled and friendly man from a top Boston clinic for disturbed children, takes me with him. He's been assigned to help the boys fix the mess they're in, and get them onto a new track. It's a heartbreaking and nearly impossible task.

When we arrive the children have already had supper and baths. Now a handful of them will talk with the psychiatrist.

Before the "Fire Setter" arrives, the psychiatrist fills me on his background. The boy's been arrested for setting fires, but he's not a pyromaniac; the fire setting is a signal for help, for a relationship of light and warmth. It seems a social worker, acting as a surrogate parent, turned up at the boy's home just in time to catch his drunken father brandishing a kitchen knife and bellowing he was going to do the kid in.

The Fire Setter, moist from his bath and in pajamas, slips through the door, climbs into the big chair by the doctor, and begins talking, nonstop, without any particular beginning or end. He, too, looks barely eight.

"Dad was just joking with the knife. He's a big joker, see. The social worker, he don't get it. It's Dad's joke, he always does that."

After the boy leaves the psychiatrist fills me in further. The boy's mother is an addict and a hooker, his father a drunken killer. The social worker saved the boy's life.

"Right now the boy can't bear to face the truth that Dad's a drunk and Mom hooks for her habit, so he has to block out all truth, because if he learns one thing he runs the risk of learning something else that maybe he doesn't want to learn. It keeps his body from growing, that's why he's so small. When he finally catches on—if he does—you'll see it first in his face. Then his body will start to grow. Right now all he can learn is a little math. Math is abstract, but reading, writing, history—any subject touching human feeling—he has to block out. He can't deal with feelings. Fires are the only way he can cry for help.

"Without someone—maybe a social worker who's willing to be a surrogate parent—he'll never learn, and chances are he'll steal a car and wind up in the Concord Reformatory (a prison outside Boston). He may well spend most of his life in and out of there. Aside from the inhumanity of it, he'll end up costing the state much more than an investment right now in social workers and psychologists who can speak the language of action."

A cop and social worker join us. The social worker rages against the local politicians: state funds allocated for highways, but nothing for children.

"When the contractors laid out Route 128, they were told to build wider bridges, but the politicians wouldn't listen. Now the state's tearing down three-year-old bridges to build wider ones, and all that money's wasted. State money goes to contractors, the politicians don't care what happens to the kids. There's no money in kids, no political glory, no votes!" The cop adds her rage.

"We can't keep them here for more than two years, we have to make room for the next batch of kids. We feed them, we teach them, we love them and we raise their hopes. Then, just when they begin to see that maybe life is ok, we have to let them go. We send them home in a new jacket, the mother takes the jacket out and sells it for drugs."

"Last month," it's the social worker again, "there was one boy we told the courts not to send him home, that something would happen, but they wouldn't listen. Before the week was out he murdered his mother."

What I carry away from that evening meeting with the psychiatrist, the social worker and the cop, is admiration for their gritty integrity, their mordant jokes, their fierce rage against feckless politicians. But more significant, I recall what the doctor said on our way home when I told him about Temple.

"If I had a kid who was autistic, I'd do what you're doing. Just improvise, figure it out as you go along."

In some fashion his remark dovetails with Temple's Viennese doctor, whose diagnosis of Temple keeps shifting and turning into questions. It even fits in with the psychiatrist who's begged me not to write about autism. One way or another, all three seem to be expressing an uneasiness with psychiatry's diagnosis of autism as a psychosocial disorder.

My last visit is to the Emma Pendleton Bradley Hospital in Rhode Island. The headmaster/psychiatrist works with severely autistic children, but will accept only a very few.

"Severely autistic children," he says, "cannot get well if they live only with other autistic children."

His teachers use the same teaching techniques for math as Dedham Country Day School. The first grade teacher helps her children learn to add columns of figures just as Mrs. Dietsch taught Temple, by bundling matches into packets of ten to illustrate "carrying" from the digit column to the tens column. What Mrs. Dietsch called "doing numbers magic." The Emma Pendleton Bradley teacher also teaches her children to recognize letters by giving them a set of wooden letters.

"If the children take the wooden letters in their hands and feel them," she says. "then they can recognize the letters on a page of print. Because they have trouble with abstracts they need that literal 'feel' in order to get the hang of reading."

I see a puzzling contradiction. The head of Emma Pendleton Bradley believes ardently in Bettelheim, which means he must believe that his severely autistic children are schizophrenic. If so, why does he feel it's medically sound, in fact preferable, to mix them in with other so-called "normal" children? And if he's right, what does that say about the private mental hospital where all the autistic children are warehoused together in the same ward?

Are Old Dazzle Bottle and Stubborn Child autistic? And the Fire Setter, his inability to recognize the threat of his father or the consequences of his fire-setting, is it, as the psychiatrist thinks, a learning block caused by parental abuse, or is he also autistic?

I see traits in the Emma Pendleton Bradley children that I associate with Temple, I think I know which of those children are autistic. But I can't get a straight take on the state children. Instead, I hear over and over in my head the last tired words of the psychiatrist as we were driving home from the state school.

"I'm tired of parents getting in an emotional bread line, expecting me to figure out and decode their autistic children. I don't know what the answer is. I haven't got the answer!"

Thus far I've only visited schools and institutions for children between eight and twelve. Because Massachusetts also sponsors educational programs to help delinquent teenagers, I'm scheduled today to visit a boys' high school on Deer Island, an island sitting in the middle of Boston Harbor. Perhaps deer once roamed it, though from the mainland dock where I'm waiting to be picked up, it looks too small for deer. Alongside of me sits a pile of provisions, also waiting to be picked up. Pretty soon, the school motor boat appears, and I climb aboard. A man stows the provisions; we cross the harbor, tying up at the Deer Island dock. I hear a halloo and see the school headmaster coming down the hill to greet me. A burly, friendly Yankee, he gives me a hand up out of the boat and orders two of his boys to unload the provisions. The boys banter with him, and I get the message right away that they like him. Better yet, they respect him. I tell the headmaster so, and he grins.

"I wasn't a top Sargent in the Marines for nothing." The headmaster's accent, with its strong, flat "r," is unmistakably New England. As he walks me up to the school, I ask how he came to be doing this job.

"I was the principal of a high school in Marblehead." Again the flat "r." "I told the parents who were sending their kids off to fancy prep schools that, if they'd contribute half that prep school tuition to their local high school, I'd use that money to raise their high school to a level competing with the best prep school. They wouldn't do it, so I figured Marblehead didn't need me. I'd go where I was needed and make my contribution there."

I ask if I can talk to the boys. He nods and introduces me to the gangly blond boy who opens the door for us.

"This is Buddy. Buddy, show her around. Hey, if she wants you to talk, you can tell her anything you feel like."

As we tour the school, Buddy admits openly that he's there because he stole a car. I think of the Fire Setter and the psychiatrist's prediction that at sixteen he'd steal a car.

"My parole officer said he'd get me off if I'd agree to come to school out here," Buddy tells me. "He said he stole a car once. It wasn't the end of the world." Buddy likes his parole officer, has a dim realization that he's been rescued, and thinks he'd like to be a parole officer himself. He worships the headmaster.

"He gives us all a fair shake. He tells me I have to make good in a job this summer, and I don't want to let him down."

Buddy talks about his old man who beats him. "When he comes home, he says 'I'm the breadwinner, I bring home the bread.' Then he acts like he's king or something, and he beats me. I don't mind it when he beats me, but I hate it when he beats my mom. Once when he did, I picked up the cat and threw it on his back. The cat clawed him, and left these big long red gashes."

Buddy laughs at his triumph. "I told my dad that was a present for my mom."

Whether Buddy has learning blocks I don't know, but I doubt it. Though his story and the Fire Setter's are essentially the same, Buddy has been able to take the measure of his father and defy him. He sees his life at Deer Island as a second chance. Will the Fire Setter be able to make that leap or will he continue to signal for help by setting fires, unable to see his act as a felony?

How many adolescents with autism end up in jail?

I visit a private school in Cambridge for privileged teenagers who've also tangled with the law but whose parents can afford to keep them out of the courts and in a special school. The headmaster observes that troubled girls are rarely arrested. The community will tolerate eccentricity, he says, but won't tolerate damage to their property, and boys damage property.

I join a class of sixteen-year-old boys with reading problems, who are slogging, painfully, boringly through a Chekhov play. The teacher asks me to read one of the roles. I give it my best dramatic shot and the boy reading opposite me immediately responds, picks up on his role and reads fluently with expression and flow. The teacher is startled. Deeply committed to analysis, her teaching technique is to stop the boy every time he stumbles on a word and ask him to explain what he thinks is the psychological reason for his stumble. Thus far, I've watched unimpressed. Perhaps the nature of the boy's problem isn't psychological; perhaps he's nervously unable. Anyway, even if the teacher turns out to be right, why would the boy want to share his anxieties with a class of his peers? There's a perverse withholding quality to the boy, as if he were deliberately keeping himself disengaged. I can see it irritates the teacher; yet, thus far, all she's given him is her intention to force him to read. Her will against his. Now he's shown her up, he's handed over his reading ability to a total stranger who's not teaching him, but enticing him with playacting.

Whatever the cause of his seeming defiance, in the brief moment of the scene reading, the boy has slipped out of his lethargy and come to life. It reminds me of singing in the vet hospitals, the times when I could see a catatonic man tapping his foot to the music. Then, as soon as the song was over how he became rigid again. I think of Temple, as a mute little girl of two, softly humming the Bach melody. Yet, when I looked at her, how she withdrew into silence.

Finally, truly baffled, the teacher lets go of her psychobabble and asks the boy outright how come he can suddenly read so well. The boy drops back into his sleepy demeanor, shrugs, avoids her eye, and murmurs, "It was interesting."

Five years from now, I'll think of the boy as a sign of the coming sixties rebellion—Bob Dylan and "the times, they are a'changing." Forty years later, I'll recognize him as Asperger's.

All through New England, there are a surprising number of private boarding schools for special teenage students. I visit as many as I can, and we film the best of them. Though much of the footage turns out to be useless for the documentary, what I learn from these schools will turn out to be far more valuable than I have any idea at the present time.

But the times, they *are* a'changing. The Beat crowd is closing in on the Leave-it-to-Beaver world, and the sixties as we will remember them, are about to begin.

August 1945 - Dick and I are engaged.

September 1947 - Temple is six weeks old.

Spring 1949 - Temple at twenty months.

Christmas 1951 - Temple is five, her sister is three.

Summer 1952 - Picnicking. In both pictures, note the position of Temple's sibling.

1952 - Temple playing with her father.

1956 - Mother's Day. Temple is on the far right.

126

Fall 1957 - School picture.

Chapter 7

The End of Childhood

Though Temple is close to entering puberty, she still yearns to go to summer camp like the rest of the Wampatuck Gang. I find a camp with top recommendations, tell the director Temple's story, and ask her please to talk to Mrs. Dietsch at Dedham Country Day School before she decides to accept Temple. All to no avail, it soon plays out.

A week after delivering Temple to the camp I get a phone call from the director. Temple's had a fever for three days, they've put her in the infirmary and given her an antibiotic.

A fever for three days and you haven't told me. Why not?

The director sweeps my question aside. Would we please come immediately and fetch Temple home.

Dick goes with me to the camp, and when we arrive we learn that, as well as the three days of antibiotics, Temple's been kept under heavy sedation.

"We had to," the director announces, voice hushed, eyes filled with shocked reproach. "She has a vaginal infection. The nurse painted it with violet gentian, and there's violet gentian on her hands. See? There's the proof. Temple touches herself.'"

Temple, groggy with drugs, can only say, "My peewee hurts." The nurse hurries to gloss over any error on her part.

"Temple's quite the little artist," she announces in a cheery voice. "Would you like to see the picture she drew for me?"

No I would not. I want to get the hell out of this witches' coven.

We drive Temple directly home to Dedham, to her own pediatrician. He says Temple has a mild infection, but that he's never seen a child so heavily sedated. Mercifully, the drugs have kept Temple too zonked to have a clear recollection of her three-day imprisonment in the camp infirmary.

It's our first family encounter with overt prejudice. Perhaps if Temple's small sin had not involved sex, the director might have been a little less Puritanically hysterical, but I doubt it. When I talk to Mrs. Dietsch, she shakes her head. She'd told the director that Temple was autistic, as had I, but clearly the director hadn't listened to a word either of us had said.

The world being what it is, perhaps something like this was bound to happen. Thus far, Temple's life has been so protected that it hasn't occurred to me to be wary of sanctimony. Dick is so angry he wants to sue the camp, but I persuade him not to, which shows the difference between us. I hide and he explodes.

I think it must be about this time that Temple asks me, "Why am I different?" She doesn't ask, "Am I different?" but "Why am I different?"

"I don't know why," I tell her, "but don't worry about it. We're each of us different, each given traits that work for us and against us. What's important is to understand the traits so you can run them, and they don't run you."

Temple appears to take this in, but in later years she'll say she

she didn't take in her difference until her teens. I think we all come to certain understandings only when we're ready to accept them. God knows I've hidden understanding from myself for years.

"I can't love," Temple announces to me suddenly.

"Love isn't all that squishy stuff, you know. All that hugging that makes you feel suffocated. That's not what love is."

"What is it then?"

"Love is wanting to make things grow: plants, animals, yourself." She looks interested. "Remember how you plant a seedling? No rough handling or you'll snap the tender shoots? And young animals. If you want the puppy to grow up to be your friend, handle him gently, so he'll know he's in a safe place."

Temple nods, remembers all too well how she yanked the puppy's ears, even though I told her not to, how finally I'd yanked her ear.

"Ow!"

"That's how the puppy feels."

"Oh." She got the message.

"The same goes for you. Love the best in yourself, treat yourself tenderly, carefully, help yourself to grow. And as you grow, you'll find you want to make the best grow in those around you. And in doing this, without really knowing why or when, we each gain a stake in the other. That's love. It's the glue that holds us together."

Temple appears to understand this, and shortly afterwards she comes to me with a confession. She and another girl have smashed an entire trash barrel of glass bottles on Mrs. Neal's garden, breaking her birdbath and leaving a welter of broken glass in the flower beds. For the first time, a little out of control and laughing her nervous laugh, Temple is deeply ashamed, in fact horrified at what the two of them have done. She doesn't know quite how they got into it. They threw a bottle at the birdbath and broke it, and from then on they couldn't seem to stop. She hopes Mrs. Neal, who is one of her teachers, won't find out that she did it. Her usual quirky indifference melts; her shame is heartfelt. She likes Mrs. Neal and wants Mrs. Neal to like her.

Once again I write to her Viennese doctor.

Often when life gets difficult for Temple, she gains an oddly mature insight about herself.

The next time I see Temple's doctor, he looks puzzled. "Why is there no sign of Temple's behavior in your other children?" he asks.

Temple's school classmate, Claudia Howlett, was born with an open heart valve. Claudia's lips are blue and her breath comes in low wheezes. She can only undertake a very quiet project, one that won't tax her doll's teaspoon of energy. Temple understands this and for the first time accepts another child's project over her own. I see the two of them in the garden setting out a pattern in the grass with leaves and flower petals.

A few years later, Claudia's heart, unequal to the task, will stop beating and her parents will establish a memorial scholarship in her name at Dedham Country Day School.

Perhaps they've known all along that Claudia's heart wouldn't be equal to the task, but I doubt it. That's not an acceptable fact.

Suddenly autism looks easy.

✳

Fall, 1961. Temple is fourteen, having a hard time of it and giving us all a hard time. Her glands are yo-yoing up and down and so is her rage. She's reached her full height and her rage carries a new strength. She pins one of the Irish girls to the wall holding her there with threats of what she can do to her if she really wants to.

"Because I'm stronger than you and I won't let you go." I see the fright in Bridie's eyes, in the siblings' eyes.

"Temple, stop it at once!" I yell, as if she were still a small child. The yell works; fortunately there's still enough of the small child in Temple to obey me. But taking into account her size, strength, and non-stop determination, I worry. Reports are coming in from school: she's a holy terror in French class. At workshop she hogs all the attention and throws a fit if she doesn't get it.

"I don't ask permission for anything," she announces when I confront her. "I go ahead and do it, and if it's wrong, too bad!"

How much is this bravado? How much is clinging to old baby ways? How much is a genuine hunger for friends and a new awareness that's she's being left out? Her classmates, on to better things, are sick of making allowances for her, and the siblings are humiliated.

"Temple is autistic when it suits her to be autistic," they say bitterly, "And she's normal when it suits her to be normal."

Later Temple tells me she's learning to substitute tears for rage. Smart enough, she says, to figure out that rage is unacceptable and tears produce sympathy. But couldn't that just be a desperate manipulation, while her rage brews away inside waiting to erupt? For now, mercifully, she seems to be able to do it, though repressing rage is a real battle, producing nerve attacks that she says are like "the worst stage fright." Also violent outcroppings of eczema on her hands which she scratches until they're raw and bleeding.

I write to Temple's doctor:

> *When Temple feels love and appreciation, her compulsive behavior dwindles, her voice loses its curious stress and she is in control of herself.... Large, noisy groups confuse her. With work she wastes a lot of energy complaining, flinging herself around, but finally buckles down to work. She wants someone near her in whom she has confidence ... in any therapy with Temple (and let us consider that your premise of psychic injury is correct)* the most important point seems to be love. As if to make up for the love she could not give or receive in her early years .... Mrs. Dietsch, Temple's teacher, feels Temple needs familiar surroundings and that those handling her should deal firmly with her eccentricities rather than being shocked by them.***

Ah, but what are the boundaries? And what is dealing firmly? Temple's hijinks at her new school now border on the unacceptable, like locking another girl in the school broom closet. In part they are to get even with the girls who tease her. Passing her in the corridor, they nudge each other and whisper, "Retard." Temple doesn't know how to join them. She's homesick for her childhood, for the days of bicycle kites and putting on plays about Bisban. Even the Wampatuck Gang is growing up. They're into boy-girl talk now and don't want any part of her "baby" projects. For the first time in her life Temple is truly bereft and the hurt of it stings to the quick. She wants back her right to be a bad sport, to be let off the hook. The timing is cruel: no more baby privileges just when she needs them most.

Despite my misgivings, she insists on wearing her "little girl" shorts to her new school. Then one day she catches sight of herself in the mirror and bursts into tears. Real tears this time, not tears substituting for rage.

"I don't want to grow up."

---

* Reference to Bettelheim's contention that autism is the result of a psychic injury caused by frigid mothering.
** Reference to the camp episode and her warning to them.

But the clock is ticking, like Peter Pan's crocodile, and we both can hear it.

The Disquieted, the documentary on disturbed children, is aired, but is not as successful as *The Innocents*. For one thing, retardation, though a tragic fact of life, is an easier subject to investigate. Autistic children can also be retarded, but the reasons for their limitations are not yet fully understood, which makes psychiatrists wary of searching questions, fearing today's answers may come back to bite them tomorrow.

But there are deeper reasons for the program's lacks. I have too big a stake in Temple's well-being to want to challenge doctors on medical choices I, myself, have been unwilling to accept. All I can manage is a fervent, heartfelt relief that Temple wasn't sucked into their vortex when she was little. I don't want to discuss her successful childhood lest the doctor's question me on her adolescence, which isn't too great right now. If any medical negativity about Temple were to find its way into the documentary, Dick would pick it up in a flash and resume his arguments. Though Dick and I continue to have our predictable fights, his present target isn't Temple, but annoyance at me for undertaking the documentary. An example, he says, of my overweening need to inject myself into everything that comes my way.

There's still another issue that keeps me silent. Sitting between the doctors and me is a two-thousand pound gorilla we don't either of us want to talk about: Doctor Bruno Bettelheim.

Bettelheim, so stunningly popular these days, recalls the dangerous and ever-present pressure of fashion on medicine, how certain doctors and remedies rise to dazzling vogue for no particular reason except that we're intrigued by them. Bettelheim's fashionableness is riding on the current movie trend of featuring psychiatrists as heroes—a trend that began twenty-five years ago with the role of Dr. Abraham Van Helsing in the thirties movie, *Dracula.*

The original publication of *Dracula,* Bram Stoker's 1897 novel, rose to fame by way of Victorian anxiety over sexual lust: an urge Victorians found deeply shocking and irresistibly present. Stoker's Dracula is an unnatural creature who can enter a lady's bedroom in any hour of the night unannounced, unexplained, yet for some godless reason always surreptitiously invited. There's no cure, but to drive a stake through him, and one, for good luck, through Mina, his favorite vampire. If you're looking for a ludicrous and titillating read, try Stoker's orgasmic rendering of Jonathan Harker thrusting a stake into Mina's heart. Again and again.

However, the thirties movie version of *Dracula* deals with something much more anxiety-making for 20th century movie goers than old style Victorian smarminess: that's the dread of neuroticism, a newly created emotional stew dreamed up by Freud and introduced to our country by European doctors with foreign accents.

We're a bit vague about what neuroticism actually is,* but we're in awe of these new doctors who call themselves psychiatrists and declare they can cure us of it. As far as we can figure out from their accented rumblings, neuroticism seems to be some kind of unwanted ego nastiness connected with infant sex. For all we know it's already entered our lives, unbeknownst and unbidden, and will contaminate our happiness if we let it get the better of us.

In a word, it's Dracula.

Dracula the egotist who lives only for himself, feeding on us in the shadows and never around in the clear morning light when it's time to shape up and be a happy person. Dracula's bite may kill us, or worse yet, turn us into something unspeakable, unacceptable ...

---

* What's the difference between a neurotic and a psychopath? A psychopath thinks 2 and 2 make 5. A neurotic knows they only make 4, but "just can't bear it."

In a word, a neurotic.

Haven't we all known people like that? Beings who suck you dry with their neediness, while they go on and on and on, forever fresh and rosy? God deliver us from being neurotic!

It isn't God who can deliver us, it's Dr. Abraham Van Helsing— the newly invented, all-knowing, all-powerful psychic authority with a foreign accent—the explainer of the unconscious, the holder-up of wolf bane. Must we tell our secret dreams to Dr. Van Helsing, the feared and revered one, so recently granted the right to pry into our souls? Yes, or he can't free us from what we keep buried during the day. By day we read about such things and try to make them seem usual, just the ordinary advances of good medicine.

But at night, when we draw the shades and see it all played out in movie shadows of black and white—No! No! No! I don't want to hear the psychiatrists sing the praises of Bettelheim! I'm not even sure I want them to clarify the subject of autism.

But then neither do they. It's a perfect symbiosis.

And who of us would dream that in another twenty years Dr. Bruno Bettelheim would turn out to be fraud?*

I reread Erik Erikson, now a seriously prominent figure in the field of psychoanalysis and human development, and am impressed all over again with his theory of identity. He's still the first to see "the ego's roots in social organization," the first to show us how our individuality is more than mere self, imprinted as it is from early childhood by family, community, city, and nation.

But since I've raised my own autistic child, since I've seen the difference between Temple and autistic children who've been institutionalized, but not much educated, I think much more positively about autism than I did when I first read Erikson. I can

---

* It will not be until 1965 that neurologists, in a study on epilepsy will stumble on the neural connections between epilepsy and autism. The first valid proof that autism is not a psychosocial disorder, reachable through psychiatry, but a bioneurological disorder.

also see how his conclusions are tied to old world Freudism, still of the school that sees autism as childhood schizophrenia, brought on by faulty maternal conditions, to be cured with talk and dosages of psychoanalysis. Yet even Erikson himself reacts to the inexplicable eerieness of autism.

> *To come face to face with a "schizophrenic" child is one of the must awe-inspiring experiences a psychotherapist can have. It is not the bizarreness of the child's behavior which makes the encounter so immediately challenging, but rather the very contrast of that behavior with the appeal of some of these children.* *

It's 1961. The suburban Leave-it-to-Beaver world and the Bebop/Beat world are still not on speaking terms, so the Leave-it-to-Beaver world still hasn't learned what the creative world has always known and accepted: the irresolvable ambiguity and ambivalence of all human life. Psychiatrists, despite doubts, are hanging onto their diagnosis of autism as a psychosocial illness, and to their role as its curer. Our suburban culture has validated psychiatry in books and movies. Psychiatrists seem to have the answer, and we like answers. We live in an economy of finished products: this year's car, this year's film, this year's cure. Finished products are so much a part of our thinking that we look for human solutions in their terms: positive commodity closure and no waffling around with "maybe." Our style is too focussed on perfection for "maybe," too quick to repair the smallest rip in the fabric of domestic bliss. We look the other way when a child is separated out, provided it's with the blessing of psychiatry.

All this being so, it's not surprising that Erikson writes without irony about the prescribed treatment of a "schizophrenic" child he calls Jean. Yet even as he describes her "faulty maternal conditions," he evidences a twinge of doubt over the diagnosis.

> *Some such maternal estrangement may be found in every history of infantile schizophrenia. What remains debatable is whether the maternal behavior could possibly be a 'cause,' for*

---

* Erik Erikson. *Childhood and Society*, Norton, NY, 1950.

such a radical disturbance in a child's functioning, or whether such children, for some intrinsic and perhaps constitutional reasons, have needs or need stimulations which no mother would understand without professional help....

Note the word "constitutional." That's the closest Erikson can come to considering the possibility of another cause. And note too, that he feels Jean's mother can't care for Jean without professional (read psychoanalytic) help. While he writes about the vital interconnection between ego and society, he sees nothing cruel or contradictory in taking six-year-old Jean away from the society of her mother and placing her in a residential psychiatric unit.**

For the first time I can see for myself that the crucial contribution to Temple's well-being has not been psychiatry, but home therapy, speech therapy, and a good private school.

December 1961. It's the week before Christmas and Christmas vacation has started. During dinner the telephone rings. Temple answers it and returns to the dinner table white-faced.

"What's the matter?" I ask.

"It was the headmaster of my school. He told me I was a menace to society."

"What!"

"He said, 'Don't come back after Christmas vacation.' And then he hung up."

"I don't believe it!"

"He didn't let me talk. He wouldn't listen to my side. He hung up on me."

---

* Erikson, Erik, *Childhood and Society*, Norton, NY, 1950.
** Recently learned through the grapevine: Jean's mother underwent psychoanalysis while Jean, encouraged by her therapists to express her rage, covered her mother with bites. Eventually Jean did acquire a little speech and was moved to a state hospital where she took long walks on the hospital grounds, circling each tree as she passed it. Now in her sixties, she lives in an institution her mother began so that her child would have some kind of permanent home.

Just like that? Just like that! He knows Temple's history, it's no secret, Temple's Viennese doctor is on his board. Why didn't the headmaster call me? We could have talked it over. We could have decided together what would be best for Temple and best for his school. How could he descend on Temple! For God's sake, she's a child! No warning, no flicker of concern for the wound he's inflicting out of his own anger.

I realize that Temple and I have both grown used to special attention at Dedham Country Day School, I realize that this is a much more grown up school, and Temple, with her temper and readiness to strike, presents a risk. But not that much risk!

I make an appointment with the Judge Baker Guidance Clinic for a conference such as we'd had with Dr. Caruthers eleven years earlier when Temple was three. I arrive to find that Dr. Caruthers is no longer there and the conference is scheduled to take place, not in a doctor's office, but in a bare hospital conference room.

The conference room windows are embedded with chicken wire, their lowered blinds let in narrow bars of winter sun and a few remote honks from the street traffic below. The room is painted pale aqua, a shade known to hospital staffs as psychopathic green, a color meant to soothe the crazed, the desperate, and me.

I sit as indicated on a solitary folding chair facing a long table with chairs behind it facing me. Two doctors I've never seen before file in and sit at the long table, followed by two interns and a social worker who carries what looks to be Temple's medical record. Where is Temple's doctor? Why does this feel like a parole board?

I am asked to tell what happened.

"Temple has thrown a book at a student in her school. The student's mother has exploded to the headmaster and the headmaster has expelled Temple."

All very cool, but inside I'm still seething over the headmaster's treatment of Temple. Was he too fearful to face his responsibility as headmaster and humanitarian, and speak to me first? No. He's removed himself the range of fire, gone AWOL and taken it out on a child.

I know Temple hasn't been too happy in her new school and I know how alarming her rages can be. But I also know the kind of teasing teenage girls go in for. For them it's a game, for Temple it's an unbearable mine field and rage is her only weapon. Stirring up her rage is what her opponents enjoy, and this time they've really gotten their kicks. Temple's exploded and been expelled. Publically humiliated before the entire school. What an outrageous triumph to grant teenage girls. I fight the nagging suspicion that the headmaster wanted to have credit with Temple's doctor, who's on his board, for accepting Temple. Now he wants an excuse to unload her.

"Don't come back after Christmas vacation."

The next day, when I'd sounded off to a member of the school board, I'd been told, quite condescendingly, how difficult Temple was, how forbearing the headmaster is. "After all, considering that Temple's autistic." But when I tell the story to Temple's Viennese doctor, for the first time I see him look discouraged. Where is he today? Why isn't he here at this conference?

The white coats at the table lean into one another and whisper sibilantly. "Autisssm, adolessscence." I can't catch the drift, but then I'm not meant to. I, too, am a felon and the parole board isn't going to let either of us go free. I wait for their opinions. I've made my bed and I can lie in it? OK, I'll lie in it, but what about Temple? Has she got to lie in it too? A whitecoat stares at me, taps a pencil against her teeth.

"What do you suggest as a solution?" I ask.

"Oh that's not really relevant. It's not what we do."

More silence, more whispers, more pencil taps.

"Could you describe Temple for us?"

Describe her? How? My chitty chatty mind goes into spasm. I could be facing the bishop. All I can think of is the church catechism, that ritual of guilty promises: "I should renounce the devil and all his works, the pomps and vanity of this wicked world and the sinful lusts of the flesh." I want to kill the row of them. I want to fling a book at the pencil lady, a heavy book with sharp corners.

"What do you propose to do about Temple?" she persists.

"Nothing at the moment." Then, determined not to let Old Doc Bettelheim get the upper hand, determined to show the whitecoats what a lovely mother I am when you get to know me, "Christmas is next week, so we thought we'd make Christmas puddings together for family presents. We've bought cut glass bowls, and raisins, and citron, and brandy, and breadcrumbs. We've put the suet through the meat grinder...."

I can't stop; my mouth has come unglued. "You have to put the suet through a meat grinder. You use it in place of lard. That's what gives the pudding its Christmas taste. That, and the brandy. Then you mix it all up and put it in the crystal bowls and you steam it, and cool it, and wrap each bowl with red cellophane...." I'm running down, I'm running lame. "It makes a lovely present."

The silence is palpable. Doesn't it dawn on the pencil lady that the week before Christmas is supposed to be a time for tidings of comfort and joy? What better thing to do with a little girl whose world has just been shattered? I want to take a shard of Christmas crystal and shove it through her cheek.

"Have you thought about a suitable school?" she asks with a lemony smile.

"Yes. I've been doing research for a television documentary on

141

disturbed adolescents. (Thank God!) I've been to all the special high schools from Maine down through Rhode Island. Out of all the schools I've interviewed, I've picked the three I like best. Temple and I have visited them and I've told Temple she can choose the one she likes best. She's old enough to have a say in her own destiny; after what's happened she's earned the right to it." I name her choice. The board is not pleased.

"We can't endorse that school. The headmaster isn't a psychiatrist. He isn't even a doctor."

I'm alert now and armed. I've finally grown up. "He's intelligent and warmhearted."

"He's a very odd man."

"Perhaps it takes a kook to catch a kook."

The board is not amused. Do they think that because I joke I take the matter lightly?

"His students care for him," I counter. "They know he's on their side. He's going to be featured in the WGBH documentary on disturbed children."

"He would be, he loves notoriety."

Notoriety. What do they think Bettelheim has been doing all these years?

Aloud I say, "He thinks it's important for the viewing public to understand the problems of troubled teenagers."

Parole is not granted.

"What school do you recommend?" I ask.

"We have a school here. It's part of the hospital." Ah, now we get to the nub. This isn't a conference, it's a sell for their own school and I've been going along with it.

"We're doctors—we're not really in the business of recommending schools."

Wait a minute, you've just recommended your own school. Aloud I ask, "Your school is here? In this crowded section of the city? Where's the playground? The grass? Hampshire Country School is in the country. It has a working farm with horses and cows."

"Well, yes, the city is a problem. But in our school we'll be able to monitor Temple."

Monitor her? How? Why would she tell you anything?

I take another leap to my maturity. Thanking the doctors, I gather up my coat, and thinking of the *Alice in Wonderland* picture of Alice rising up amid the playing cards, fight the urge to dismiss them all in Lewis Carroll's words:

"Who cares for you? You're nothing but a pack of cards!"

At my rising, faces close, notebooks snap shut. The dust motes dance in the sun bars and there's a general looking at watches. The meeting has been a competition of wills and for the first time I know that I know more than these doctors. If anybody is going to "monitor" Temple, it will be me.

We parade down the metal stairs in silence. Nobody wishes well for Temple, nor do they show the faintest sign of caring.

I walk behind the whitecoats, mentally adding up what their years of psychiatric training have cost them in grinding study, burnout fatigue, endless loans, and shabby gentility. And as for you two pasty interns walking last in line, more years of it yet to come, boys. Count the years ahead of you before you'll finally climb up into that catbird seat where, right or wrong, your psychiatric counseling will turn to gold.

I go home and talk to Temple. She, too, has reached a new sense of resolve, recognizing finally that her baby pranks, like her little girl shorts, are unworthy of her. She has not been excused as she would have been once upon a time when she was little. She's walking away, head high and dignity intact, in full acceptance of her actions and their cost. But she's also walking away from a mean adolescent game, for which she has neither the ammunition nor, thank God, the appetite. She's made of better stuff than that, and in time she'll prove it.

Christmas comes and goes. The first week in January Temple and I pack up her belongings for a new start in a new school of her own choosing, a small school in New Hampshire for teenagers with special problems. The headmaster is a kindly, older version of the burly Deer Island headmaster.

We stow her gear in the car and set off, up the narrow roads, through woods filled with laurel bushes that will be in bloom on later trips. Where one New England mill town leaves off, the next begins, each with its red brick factory hanging over the riverbank as it has for a hundred years.

Soon the towns thin out, the houses thin out. We hit farm country, turn in at a white wooden gate and drive up the dirt road to Hampshire Country School.

The school has a working farm with cows and pigs and, to Temple's delight, horses to ride. She doesn't know it yet, but Mr. Carlock, the science teacher, will become her beloved mentor, guiding her to a lifelong love of science.

I visit Temple's school often and sometimes take Temple and her roommate out to dinner. Temple cautions me not to smack my lips during dinner, that her roommate can't stand the sound of it. For the first time she's concerning herself with somebody else's peace of mind.

I grow fond of both Mr. Patey, the headmaster, and his wife. An older man, intuitive and perhaps a bit eccentric, Mr. Patey runs his Hampshire Country School with a loose rein and is surprised by nothing. In the evening after Temple is in her dorm for the night, I sit with the Pateys in their kitchen, talking long hours, Mr. Patey guiding me to a deeper understanding of autism.

One afternoon Temple and I watch the school farmer help one of his cows give a breech birth to her calf. Unable to deliver, the cow lies on her side, the legs of the unborn calf protruding from her, the rest wedged in her birth canal. Not about to lose either the cow or the calf, the farmer knots a hemp rope around the unborn legs, braces his foot against a barn post and hauls on the rope with all the brawn his back can support. Nothing budges, not the cow, not the calf. Again he hauls, and again—long, hard, sweaty pulls. The cow makes no sound, the barn is still save for the creak of the barn post. Then without fanfare, just as the farmer is easing up on the rope, the calf slides backwards into the world. The cow lifts her head and licks it. The calf wobbles to its feet, stands rocking for a moment, then steadies itself for life on its own.

Whatever the future holds, I know Temple is safe.

Where does Dick stand on Hampshire Country School? He's accepted it for the moment and is prepared to pay its stiff tuition. But he's chewing on the inside of his cheek these days, and has cut me off from the funds his father gives annually to each daughter-in-law. A sure sign that he sees me as a poor invest-ment. From now on, despite his protestations of love, he will keep me on a very short financial leash.

March 1962. Temple's Viennese doctor stares down at the note-book in front of him, those pages incised once again with Dick's familiar cramped cursive. What do they say now? What is the doctor reading and reading in? Once again fear and guilt clot in my belly as they did twelve years ago when first we met. I thought we two had come through the worst of it, reached an understanding, a kind of friendship. Dizzy with anxiety, I fight the indignity of fainting. Why have I been summoned to meet with him alone? What have I done now?

The doctor looks at me, his head slightly tilted, his mouth with its faint sneer that I can never interpret. He chooses his words as he might select a morsel from a passing tray of hors d'oevres.

"Mrs. Grandin," he says—the hors d'oevres are clearly unappetising—"Are you aware that Mr. Grandin is trying to prove that you are insane?"

I stare, shocked.

"That he has been keeping a notebook on you for the past three years?" He flips the pages in front of him. "Every move you have made."

The faintness vanishes. Three years of spying, watching me like a mole! Writing it all down and reporting it to the doctor! Why? What are the two of them cooking up? Three years—God knows what can be culled from the suburban mishmash of daily living. Does the doctor see me as an unfit mother? For an instant I wonder if I'm mad. Is this what madness is? Inquisitor and prisoner, the doctor and I face each other alone in his soundproof office. What are we talking about? What am I on trial for? Four children are riding on me.

"Mrs. Grandin." The Doctor's sibilance cuts in. "I think you better leave your marriage, and I think you better leave as quickly as possible."

For a moment I'm deaf to the import of what he's saying. All I can feel is the basement chill of his office.

"I do not like to testify in court, but I have done it before and I will do it again. If your husband tries to take you to court, I will testify to your sanity."

The chill vanishes. The doctor continues in his brittle way.

"I understand that you have been seeing a psychiatrist, yourself. May I have your permission to talk to him?"

"Of course."

The next time I see my own shrink, he tilts back in his creaky leather chair, his love of drama coloring his tale. It seems the two doctors, after consulting together, called Dick in and announced that should he try to take me to court to prove I'm insane, they are both going to testify against him.

"Dick left my office screaming, 'All you goddam psychiatrists! You're no goddam good!'"

Those two doctors, they're my Sanity Clause.

Years later it finally will dawn on me that Temple's doctor was indeed an Austrian Jew who escaped the Nazis, that he had recognized in the notebook a dangerously obsessive mindset, and understood the importance of rapid departure.

How much it must have cost this stiff little man with his faintly sneering mouth, to swallow his Viennese pride and conclude that he'd seen Dick the wrong way around, that he and his colleagues had summed up autism the wrong way around, and that, perhaps, he had looked at me the wrong way around.

The last time I saw him, he rose from his power chair. "Mrs. Grandin, you have done a job that has put the entire staff of Children's Hospital to shame. Do you realize it is as rare as if Temple had recovered spontaneously from leukemia?"

I treasure his words. His blessing.

August 1962. Dick and I are divorced, and I receive full custody of all four of our children. It's a huge release, carrying with it deep distress. I know the good man Dick wants to be, and is in part, and could be if the cards had fallen differently. And I know that I'm taking away his happiness. Somehow our conflict shouldn't have reached such an appalling, head-on collision, but it has. I am too young, too green, too frightened, too angry to sort out my own wild plunges at life from what I see as important for Temple. And Dick is too impatient to listen.

Yet the story shouldn't end on such a final and crushing note. Years from now I may be able to unravel what happened and why. But I can't now.

Now I can only see as far as Temple's mastery over the first hurdles of autism. And in the process of recalling them I've found my own coming of age. But those two stories are in part—a tragic part—Dick's story. Autism became his nemesis, the wellspring of our endless, headstrong controversies. Have I done him an injustice, dwelling on his rage, his folly, honor upheld, and hopes dashed? Or have I only told my version of the family secrets, sung to my *con disperazione* tempo?

Each time I try to sum it up, the past darts away from me—fireflies in the summer dusk. Someone else may be quick enough to catch one and put it in a jar and for a brief moment it might give out its uncanny fire. But the trapped light dims, the creature in the jar is never quite the same.

Yet the private moments of our family life keep right on sparking. There, over there, see them in the grass? Ping pong matches on rainy afternoons, the flying horses at Oak Bluffs, another over there, miniature golf and nonsense names for the children. More, more, late Christmas Eve, Dick and I secretly stuffing the children's stockings. One blazing August noon, Dick and I spotting a whale circling our boat, laughing as we watch it watching us, rolling and wheezing in the sunny chop of Cape Cod Bay.

The moments dart about in fiery swarms, their insect lanterns wink and flash—then suddenly they're gone—and I must go too—and I'm taking the children—

I'm so sorry.

Chapter 8

Then What Happened?

Not without trauma, we move on. Temple is safe and happy at Hampshire Country School, the siblings and I are ok, but sadly, a new and serious lack of funds makes it imperative to dismiss the two dear Irish girls. We all miss them ferociously, particularly my youngest.

The Leave-it-to-Beaver world walks politely around me. No one so much as telephones. Dick, now single, is wined, dined and sought after by every hostess in Boston.

I run into Al Capp on Brattle Street. The Capps live in Cambridge and Al is a big shot in the Poets Theatre. I dump all the bad stuff of my life on him, and feeling sorry for myself, break my rule against weeping. Al hands me his silk paisley handkerchief, which produces more tears.

"I can't blow my nose in thaaaaat! It's siiiilk."

Unimpressed, Al says in his nasal drawl: "Honey, start again. Don't be one of those wistful types. Don't say Paris must be lovely. Go there and find out." And off he stumps on his artificial leg.

Since I'm still silenced by damaged vocal chords, I figure I'd better pick up where I left off on my education sixteen years earlier. I visit my old Radcliffe dean, who arranges for me to take less than a full academic load. A first for Harvard.

"It took some convincing," she and another dean tell me. "But we finally persuaded the Harvard deans that the care of four children was the workload equivalent of two courses." At that, the two of them throw back their heads and roar with laughter. "You're our guinea pig. If it works, we're going to let other mothers do it."

Professor Harry Levin recognizes me from a Harvard Dramat production of *Much Ado About Nothing,* seventeen years earlier, and takes me into his graduate Shakespeare seminar. I submit an essay to Professor Theodore Morrison who takes me into his creative writing class. It's from him that I learn about the thorn in Robert Frost's pocket, an image I'll carry with me the rest of my life.

Every morning the children and I leave for school at 8:30 a.m. and return home at 4 p.m., have early nursery supper, and do our homework together around the dining room table. The children all pull up their marks at school, and I feel like an old lilac bush that's been cut back and fed.

My day student costs, including books and gas, come to $1,000 a year. Hard to believe today.

I wish I could say that Temple pulls up her marks at Hampshire Country School, but in truth she doesn't do any school work at all. Instead she rides horses and mends bridles. Mr. Patey feels that Temple needs this freedom so she can find her way to a new emotional equilibrium, and respectful of his judgement, I agree. Adolescence is hard enough for any child, but autistic adolescence is something devised by the devil.

In 1965 I graduate from Harvard, marry Ben Cutler and move to Bronxville, New York. Ben is from New England and, like me, a rebel from the ranks of Waspdom. The product of Andover and

Yale, he moved to New York as soon as he'd graduated from Yale, and parlayed his musical talents into a career as a popular "society" band leader in the style of Peter Duchin. Ben's affection for Temple is open and positive. One of his children matches one of mine in age and interests. So I've suddenly acquired, along with a new husband, an extended family. A joy I'd never envisioned.

The siblings love their new life, and most of the Bronxville High School seems to take up residence with us.

Our Bronxville house had once been the carriage house and stable on an old estate. The horse stalls and stable roof had been torn down leaving the bricks of the stable floor to form an open courtyard. But the surrounding garden was still enclosed by a high stone wall with iron rings embedded in it. The rings must have been used to hold the horses before unbridling them and leading them back to their stalls.

Now that we haven't the money for the full professional renovation that the house needs, we work on the house as a family project, led by Rudy Anderson, a superb local carpenter who constructs the major renovations. I attribute my children's building know-how, including Temple's—she works with us during school vacations—back to this period. The rest of their lives, all four children will be constructive, in every sense of the word.

All four will also be visualizers. While still in her teens, my youngest child will emerge as a fine artist, her paintings winning their first attention in a town exhibit.

Temple has already written about her summers with "Aunt Brecheen." Ann Brecheen, now dead, was Ben's sister. One day, when Ben and I were visiting her in Arizona, we came up with the idea that Ann's ranch would be the perfect place for Temple to summer. And so it proved. Ever since her summer with Ann,

Temple has loved the West. As well as being a rancher, Ann was a teacher, librarian, and charmer.

I take up teaching drama at the Westchester School of Music and Theatre. I also write school lessons for the television networks. The lessons, geared to specific TV programs, and called "Teacher's Guides," are coordinated to school curricula and sent to all USA high schools.

The next summer vacation Temple and I start in on covering the kitchen walls with four-by-eight panels of composition walnut siding. We buy the siding, are congratulating ourselves on how well it goes with the rest of the house—kind of an old world library-cum-kitchen effect—when, oops! We discover we're two sheets short on the siding. By this time I'm up on a ladder gluing acoustic tiles into the ceiling and don't want to stop.

"Temple, you're free. Drive down to Webers and buy us two more sheets of siding."

"I can't."

"Why not? Of course, you can."

"No, it'll make me nervous and I'll cry, and then what will the boy behind the counter think?"

"What do you care what the boy behind the counter thinks? He's just some jerk selling lumber and you'll never see him again. Cry, and buy the siding anyway." Off she goes. Omigod, have I asked too much? After what feels like an eternity I hear the car pull into the drive. The siding is tied to the roof and Temple is triumphant.

"I cried and bought it anyway!"

Fall rolls round, Temple returns to school and wakes up to the fact that if she wants to go to college, she'll have to settle down to some solid academic work. Guided by her science teacher, Mr.

Carlock, she catches up to where she should be, graduates from school, and is accepted into Franklin Pierce, a recently established college close to Hampshire Country School. However, it should be noted that all this takes some doing.

Temple's decision to progress from non-student to student is motivated by her fixation on her cattle chute/squeeze machine (more on that later), and her fierce determination to prove its value scientifically. Noting this, Mr. Carlock points out to Temple that, if she wants to achieve her goal, she'll have to study college science. And, in order to get into college, she'll have to graduate from high school. And in order to graduate from high school, she'll have to fulfill the academic requirements that, up until now, she's chosen to ignore.* Once the steps are clear, Temple sets to work, her fixation on her cattle chute motivating her to trudge through the courses that don't hold her interest. Hampshire School tutors her to graduation, and Mr. Patey helps her to be accepted at Franklin Pierce.**

Franklin Pierce turns out to be a blessing: friendly and flexible. Temple can visit Mr. Patey and Mr. Carlock whenever she feels the need or the mood. Once again, she discovers that, if she wants her classmates to respond to her project, providing her with the research data she needs for the validation of her cattle chute, she'll have to take an interest in their projects. I keep in touch with her progress through her dean at Franklin Pierce. He likes Temple and wants her to succeed but is worried about her inability to do math.

"It will be a problem if she goes to graduate school." He knows Temple wants to do that. He also understands that she's autistic.

This kind of intense "special accommodation" teamwork, both at Hampshire Country School and Franklin Pierce College, is rare for the sixties. It will only begin to be accessible forty years later when Marshall University in Huntington, West Virginia, will offer college level assistance for bright young students who

---

* Today Temple notes the importance of using the restrictive interests of an autistic person to motivate him into serious study.
** Hampshire Country School was a hands-on school with high ratio of teachers and psychologists to students. In effect, it was private tutoring far in advance of its time.

are struggling with autism.

Four years later, all of us, including Dick, go to Temple's Franklin Pierce graduation. When the diplomas are given out, Temple receives top honors: magna cum laude, second in a class of four hundred. I'm ecstatic. Dick accepts "proud father" congratulations a bit stiffly. Four years earlier, as soon as Temple had graduated from Hampshire Country School, he'd tried to arrange for her to live in a private emporium for the dull witted.

After seven years of feeling as if there's a fish hook lodged in my throat, I wake up one morning to find, when I swallow, that the fish hook is gone. Have the blood vessels in my vocal chords actually healed? Is it possible? I go to a doctor, who grabs my tongue, peers down my throat at my vocal chords, and says, "Yes, completely healed!"

I take a summer stock role to see if my speaking voice will hold up. Then, very cautiously, resume singing under the tutelage of a New York voice teacher and coach. Music is a big part of our lives now. Ben and his various bands are not only much sought after for weddings and dances, but Ben also books bands into prestige hotels like the Broadmoor in Colorado Springs, the Elbow Beach in Bermuda, and the Pierre in New York.

What happens next is glorious serendipity.

At four o'clock on a Saturday afternoon, the girl singer at the Pierre calls Ben to say that her child is ill and she can't make the gig. Ben looks at me.

"It's too late to book any of the regular singers. Do you think you can swing it?"

Yes, yes, yes.

"OK, it's yours. Be sure to sing some French songs, they love that French stuff at the Pierre."

In I go, and sing the night away, where, by a lucky fluke, the manager of the Pierre is having dinner with friends. On Monday morning the manager calls Ben.

"Your wife sings beautifully. And in French, too. Would she be willing to take the off nights?" (Off nights are Sunday and Monday.)

Yes, yes, yes.

My next hurdle is Stanley Worth, the Pierre band leader. He's not as ready as the manager to accept me. Nor is the piano player, whose only remark is, "Well, at least you look like a singer."

However, the manager is the manager, so Stanley has to tolerate me, and I improve. After a few weeks, at the close of one night, there's a rap on my dressing room door. It's Stanley. He gives a nod and says, "You'll do."

I love the long hours of the Pierre job, and drive home each night singing at the top of my lungs. The lyrics that I write a few years later will come, I know, from those nights. Music is a different experience when you're inside the harmony and rhythm. The men play their own variations on whatever pop song I'm singing. So from now on, I listen for a wonderful little counter melody that Stanley likes to play against "S'Wonderful."

I call Professor Morrison in Cambridge to talk about the job, and his response is literary. "Ha! What yarns you'll have to tell!"

After singing in the Pierre, Ben's drummer suggests that Ben book me to sing on his big band jobs. Singing with the four Pierre men is a delight, but singing with a twenty-two piece band is frightening. I sit in front of three saxes, each sax blasting a different note in my ear till I lose all sense of where we are in the music. Now it's my turn to sing. I have only the end of the last song chorus and the pick-up notes to the repeat, in which to signal the leader my key change,* get up to the mike, turn it on, and hear my key change. All this, along with a prayer that I come in with the right note on the right count.

After band singing I begin writing and performing songs and comedy on my own—very late sixties style—finally accumulating enough material to consider undertaking a full cabaret act. Frank Wagner, choreographer for Radio City Music Hall, helps me put the act together. An act is different from stage acting in that there's no role to hide behind. You have to engage directly with the audience. I find that more terrifying than the twenty-two piece band.

Frank is not impressed. "Stop acting as if it doesn't matter whether or not they like you," he growls, "If you ignore them and keep pretending they aren't there, they won't give a hoot about you or your act." Frank pries me out of the dressing room where I'm waiting to go on. "Stop hovering back there! Go out in the bar and make friends! Talk to anybody!" Advice that will prove invaluable when it comes time to lecture to autism societies.

I perform in various New York cabarets; I also work for the cabarets, auditioning and introducing their other acts. At the same time, I continue to teach drama at the Westchester Academy of Music and Theatre. Most of the students are in their twenties, with a smattering of late teenagers. Once in a while I get a twelve-year-old, but one particular child looks to be no more than seven. His grandfather, a bulky, white-haired man, brings him to me, looking at his grandson with his heart in his eyes. "I want my grandson to learn there's no people on earth better than show people." The man tells me that for years he was a high wire circus performer and reels off a series of names. Do I know them? Have I seen them on the high wire?

I haven't.

"I caught them all, I was their catcher." The names must be impressive, because he adds, "I caught the greats."

---

* Because of the sound volume on the band stand, key changes are signalled by fingers. Up for the number of flats, down for sharps. Key of C, a "C" with forefinger and thumb.

I look at this man, his sturdy frame softened with age to the shape of a pear. He looks no more fit to perform on a high wire than a retired plumber. Yet once upon a time, the strength in those arms must have been great enough to catch another performer in mid-flight. And talk about precision. Over and over he had to be there for those greats he was so proud of catching. And always in the split second swing of the trapeze.

He leaves his grandson with me, and after a short workout, I can see that the boy's extraordinarily talented.

Since he's too young to work with the adult members of the class, I make up a monologue for him from the first scene of *Dark of the Moon*, a play about a witch boy who longs to be human. I give it to him to take home.

"Learn it by heart for the next lesson."

In acting, there's what's called "sensory recollection," which is, quite simply, finding an emotional moment in your own life that matches the one in the play, and using your recall of it to fulfill the scene. Easy to explain, hard to do.

When the boy comes for his next lesson, it's 5:30 in the afternoon and already dark. Classes are mostly in my living room because it's larger than the school studio. I tell the boy that his character, the witch boy, has to travel a long, frightening journey to get to the conjur man whom he hopes will make him human. And it's only because he hopes, even though he's scared, that he has the courage to make the trip.

"I have an idea to help you get into the witch boy's heart. There's a mailbox at the end of our path. See that path out there? It goes down those stone steps through the woods. The woods are dark now, full of dry leaves and rustlings and creaky branches. I'll put the light on in the house, so you can see me in the window. Do you think you're brave enough to go down to that mailbox alone and then come back up the hill alone?"

The boy nods and goes out the door. Omigod, again have I asked too much? I watch him out the window. I know, firsthand, just how scary that path can be at night. The boy makes it up the path, comes in the door, his eyes round.

"Now can you ask the conjur man to make you human?" Eyes still round, the boy starts in.

"I gotta see you, conjur man, I gotta ask you something." He gulps and goes on. "Conjur man ... Listen to me ... I come a long way ... I been askin' and askin'...."

He's magic.

The acting technique of using sensory recollection and empathy to get inside a character, will in time lead me to understanding something of what's missing in people with autism.

For now I'd like to pick up on what happened to Temple after Franklin Pierce. For those who've not read Temple's book, here in her own words is the gist of her next steps:

"I wanted to do my master's thesis [Arizona State University] in animal science on the behavior of cattle in feedlots in different types of cattle chutes.... My master's thesis brought together all of my ideas about and fixations on the way things work."*

After some demurral on the part of the Arizona State University faculty—in 1974 animal behavior research was a rarity— Temple's project was finally honored. "After all," Temple writes, "if I hadn't used the squeeze chute on myself I might not have wondered how it affected cattle."

Temple's squeeze machine is something she first built at Hampshire Country School, developed further at Franklin Pierce, wrote about in her dissertation, and to this day climbs into for

---

* Temple Grandin. *Thinking in Pictures*, Vintage Books, 1995.

relaxation. In essence, it's a chute used for holding cattle in a gently squeezing position in order to calm them for inoculation and branding. While still a teenager at Ann Brecheen's ranch, Temple had crawled into one and discovered that it's gentle pressure gave her the tender hugging she'd always wanted but couldn't bear to accept because any hugging, including her mother's, made her profoundly anxious. Here, suddenly, miraculously, was a mechanical hug she could administer to herself by herself and for herself. Nothing would do but to build her own cattle chute, and ever since, the squeeze machine has been both her source of good feeling and a lifelong fixation. While working for her M.A., Temple began writing for the *Arizona Farmer Ranchman,* which led her to designing cattle chutes for Corral Industries. From Arizona she went on to the University of Illinois for a doctorate in animal science.

Today, Temple is internationally known for her animal slaughtering systems. She counts McDonald's, Burger King, Wendy's, and KFC among her customers. Now that she's an Associate Professor of Animal Behavior at Colorado State University, well-recognized for her research on the breeding and handling of livestock, she's also in a position to advise these companies—she advises 90% of the U.S. meat packing industry—on the humane treatment of the creatures they're about to slaughter. No small feat!

But more important, Temple is world famous for her triumph over autism. Oliver Sacks has written about her, calling her "An Anthropologist on Mars," the description Temple gave him of herself when they first met. Today she says she still feels as if she existed on an alien planet where she must, like a good anthropologist, figure out through conscious observation and logic why we, its inhabitants, behave the way we do. Though autism still robs Temple of the spontaneous interplay most of us come equipped with from birth, by watching us closely and figuring out the why's and how's of our behavior, she's achieved an amazing facsimile of it. Not a cure for her autism, but her own self-developed understanding of our social interaction. Over the years she's become so adept at it that sometimes it's hard for people to know whether her reactions spring from a consciously imposed pattern or an innate response.

In 1999, Temple, now in her fifties and an autism celebrity, asked me to join her on the autism lecture circuit.

"Mother, families with autistic children want to hear you. They want to know what magic you did to help me."

"There was no magic," said I modestly, my vanity purring like a satisfied tabby. "I just did the best I could." At that My Own Personal Past, forever a sloppy young puppy, sighed and rolled over, the metal tag on its collar giving out a reproachful chink.

"No, I'm not going to let you out. I'm snug and warm now, Temple doesn't need my help anymore, in fact she's way ahead of me." The Past tried to go back to sleep as commanded, but could only flop about and whimper. Finally, unable to bear it any longer, it pushed its baby muzzle into my lap.

"All right, I'll let you out, but I won't let you off the leash." With that I told Temple I'd go with her to an autism conference and try my luck at giving a lecture. Once the door opened, The Past sprang out dragging me with it, and almost immediately we were joined by The Present, an elderly, rump-sprung retriever, who began at once to sniff and nudge at both of us. The puppy, being a puppy, wanted to romp, the retriever, being a retriever, wanted to retrieve, and I, desperate for control, wanted to hang onto the leash.

"Stop it, both of you!" I yelled, but it was too late. The Past and The Present were scampering hither and yon, the leash was a joke, and before I knew it, I was lecturing to Autism Societies in over half the United States, as well as Canada, Bermuda, Ireland, Hong Kong and the U.K.

Lecturing soon nudged open a door I thought I'd shut tight

forty years earlier. After Temple graduated from Franklin Pierce I never explored autism again, but when parents started asking me questions, heartbreaking questions, I found I had no up-to-date answers. Then, too, there'd been a huge medical turn-around since Temple was a child, and the old interpretation of autism as a psychosocial disorder had gone the way of the dodo. Now recognized as a neurological disorder, the diagnosis of autism had broadened to include everything from nerdy Ph.D.'s, mystified by social chitchat, to those so severely afflicted they couldn't talk at all.

In addition, something new had entered the picture: how the extreme traits of autism play out in "shadow" form in preceding members of the family. Would this mean I'd have to learn how the combination of Grandin/Purves genetic traits may have created Temple's autism? What about how they played out in our own lives?

Medical facts would prove readily accessible, but not so the past. Insight into the past didn't arrive in any logical sequence, nor in blinding flashes and Joycean epiphanies. At first, the picture was faint, but like a negative floating in its emulsion, the past slowly emerged. Even then it wasn't something I could perceive deliberatively, but rather something I'd have to allow to accumulate in its shadowy bath. There was something ghostly about the process.

I've always felt that ghosts were unfulfilled motives and actions, left hanging in the air after death. An incompletion so strong that in certain favored spots it can still disturb the air waves, waiting there to be recognized and released by a living empathy.

Our old Bronxville house had a ghost.

In long summer evenings when the blue twilight seemed to hold forever, I used to garden in the brick courtyard, filling my watering can from a faucet in the back entry where there was an ancient flight of stairs. Originally they must have led up to groom's quarters above the space where the carriages were kept.

One evening in the dusk I came into the back entry with my watering can and was suddenly aware of a man's presence. And of a strong smell of cigar smoke. It didn't frighten me. Instead I had the feeling the presence was entertained I'd found it. I felt the man's laughter.

Off and on, over a period of two or three years, I was conscious of this presence—always in the summer, always at the hour of blue dusk, always the smell of cigar smoke. I told the children, but they were never around at the right moment. It was summer and they'd be off with friends. Alone, I grew comfortable with the presence, even came to expect it.

When you live in an old house people are always coming around to see what the place looks like now. One summer afternoon my children called up the stairs, "Mom, there's a man outside who wants to see the house."

The man, in his seventies, said he was the minister's son and as a boy had lived at the bottom of our hill where the church rectory was.

"We used to play up here when it was a working stable. The groom, John Damon, was a great guy; he didn't mind us hanging around him. Automobiles had just come in, and Mr. Chambers, the owner, had bought one. John was good with the horses, but he was crazy about that motorcar. Always tinkering with it. But then something happened, I've never forgotten it. One summer evening, John was underneath the car fixing something when the block holding up the car slipped, and the car came down on him. He was so strong, he held the car off while we ran for help, but by the time we got back it was too late. He was dead."

I showed the minister's son around inside, and when we came to the back entry, he said, "John had quarters up those stairs."

My children looked at me. "Mom, it's your ghost."

I think it was, and I think the minister's son released it, because I never felt the presence again.

Somehow, John Damon needed us to know his story.

There's something of the same ghostliness in learning about family genetics. Physical inheritance is easy: "Oh, he has your blue eyes." But the traits of disposition, how they play out in the next generation, are far more elusive. Doctors refer to them as "shadow" traits, meaning traits not pronounced enough to disturb the ordinary surface of life. But what an oddly emotional way to define a trait that is, quite simply, not in an extreme form.

Researching the present state of autism, understanding how its genetics relate to all humanity, past and present—including Dick's and mine—has been a humbling and somewhat ghostly experience. Autism isn't an exotic disorder, out there somewhere on its own, the fault of mercury or inoculations, waiting to be "cured" if we throw enough money at it. Autism is an exaggeration of what lies in us all.

And studying it has been my form of exorcism.

In September 1999, Temple introduced me to Wayne Gilpin, the president of Future Horizons, an organization presenting autism conferences, nationally and internationally. Wayne persuaded me to give a lecture for Future Horizons and held out a trip to the U.K. as bait. It was too good to resist. But then came the question: what will I say to those English mothers who will have traveled so far, trundling their desperations before them? Like everything else about autism and the past, what to say emerges slowly, starting for me on a hot afternoon in Slough, England.

It's the tag end of summer and for an English afternoon, insufferably hot. The first two speakers have already presented their lectures, and now comes a short tea break. Nervous tedium fills the airless, low-ceilinged, second floor lecture hall. The mothers drape their sodden jackets over chair backs and exchange joky, chin-up platitudes about the weather. I beg the building manager to open a window.

"This is a municipal building," he protests. "It is air conditioned, can't you feel it?"

No, not really. There's one more speaker before I'm on, so I go downstairs to sit by the open front door, and figure out how I'll start off my lecture.

"Know that you and your child will come through." Yes, that's how I'll begin.

"You'll know more, feel more—be awed, puzzled, scornful of sentimentality and less willing to accept the obvious." True, but don't the words sound pompous?

Maybe I should come right out with it, and talk about the screaming fits, the spitting, the pitying glances of other children's mothers at birthday parties, and the everlasting guilt gnawing away on you. Yes, and panic.

"You and your child will roll in the undertow, sand-filled breakers slamming you forward, sucking you back, scraping your knees raw, filling your eyes, your nose, your mouth with gritty salt water." Then what?

"You'll survive, that's what. You'll find your footing and stagger up onto dry land holding on tight to your child. You'll limp but you'll make sense. There'll be good days and nightmare nights, moments of great pride and days when you want to slink out of sight. But it won't be raw knees in the undertow."

Too self-indulgent and self-pitying. Try another.

"I'm here, that's what matters. Survival is a statement, a conviction that the game is worth the candle. I've learned to love the game, learned to climb up and peer into the machinery of it, all oily and glorious and irrelevant—wheels wobbling, sand spewing into the gears, pistons squeaking up and down at cross purposes. Amazing. Somehow the whole Rube Goldberg contraption works."

But these ladies are English. Will they get that? Maybe I should be more literary.

"All of us when we hear the news, the official diagnosis, our reaction is shock. 'You mean my child won't be able to handle everyday life? Ever? Is that what you're telling me?' No! It's not true!"

"Grief, rage, guilt, denial—it all courses through us. Then comes the next shock. We, the parents we thought we were, in a world we thought we understood, have in a single moment, become painfully and permanently changed.

"Identity. That vital and fragile core of our being, born of moments when we feel the most ourselves, acquired consciously and unconsciously over the course of our years, slowly visible to us and to the world while at the same time being shaped by us and the world."

"That's not like you, a friend says. And we agree. Or perhaps we say nothing and think to ourselves, That's all you know!" Either way, another layer of identity is laid down.

"But what of the identity of our child who, we've just learned, is autistic? A child whose take on the world physically, socially and emotionally is distorted by a sensory scrambling neither we nor the doctors fully understand? Is that why she can't speak? Can't bear to be touched? How will we talk to each other? How will we live without touching each other? My baby who can't bear to look into my eyes? And here's the catch. A baby needs a mother to know she's a baby. But a mother needs a baby to know she's a mother. The sensory scrambling facing my child is reinforced by the emotional scrambling facing her parents.

"When the usual responses can't grow, consciously and unconsciously, a whole family is changed."

Yes, that's more like it.

A wedding party of Sikh Indians in full regalia is making an entrance through the open door next to where I'm sitting. They've come for an English civil service marriage prior to their own wedding ceremony.

Two grandfathers parade in, white-bearded and brilliantly turbanned. How Victorian London must have adored India, that exotic jewel they stole for their queen's crown. Next comes an ancient grandmother, her orthopedic shoes sticking out from under her best sari. Then the groom, a blue turban setting off his glossy black beard. Last the bride, story-book beautiful, her red silk, gold trimmed sari rippling in a halo over her long black hair, her perfect features set off by a gold caste mark.

Applause leaks down the stairway, overhead I can hear chairs being pushed back. Fifteen minutes and it's my turn to speak. I gather up my notes, I know what I want to say.

As I go up the stair, I take a last look at the story book couple and wonder what will be their future? They look so like an Edmund Dulac illustration for *Bluebeard*.

After an introduction, I tell the English mothers the first truth I'd stumbled on, all those years ago: if I didn't survive, Temple wouldn't survive. Somehow, we'd both have to grow up. I to raising Temple along with my puppy self. Temple to learning to act like a normal citizen of this planet. But that led to the question: what is normal and normal for what? Hard on its heels came another question: why had I been unwilling to act on the fifties diagnosis that Temple was an "infant schizophrenic" when her father and the rest of the world accepted it?

Well, when I look back, I see that my so-called brave stand wasn't really all that brave, or all that clear. No doctor ever directly recommended institutionalizing Temple, neither Dr. Caruthers, nor Temple's Viennese doctor. Perhaps doctors in those years didn't recommend that sort of thing straight out, but waited for a parent to suggest it? I remember when neighbors asked me what autism was, I'd say "infant schizophrenia," and feel a inward shudder. Even with that, I didn't take in the full implication of what I was saying. Instead the words felt vaguely aggrandizing of Temple's oddity, important enough to make her more acceptable to the neighbors. Putting Temple in an institution never crossed my mind, nor did I ever dream that Dick would seriously go that route.

But as soon as I've considered that absurd old dream, I recall Dick's ceaseless intention to do just that. Even after Temple had graduated from an accredited high school, he was still trying to arrange for her to go to a classy home for the retarded. How could I have ever been blind to his intention? But I was. That's the oddity of denial. In those days we didn't talk openly about personal matters, it wasn't considered the thing to do. With a subject as touchy as Temple's autism, neither Dick nor I ever allowed the words to surface.

That I didn't take in fully either Dick's intention, nor the "infant schizophrenia" label, was probably lucky. There's something to be said on the side of denial, particularly when one is an immature twenty-two. The world I'd been reared in, the world I married into, didn't ask for much from me but social grace. Talent, curiosity, and passion weren't encouraged, in fact were actively discouraged. The old Victorian saying, "Be good, sweet maid, and let who will be clever," still reigned in the "cold roast" Boston of my young years. Nevertheless, the label's brutal slap left its mark.

From early babyhood when Temple didn't like to be touched, she appeared to be bored with my attempts to play with her, and as a result, made me feel snubbed and rejected. Had Temple been born later in the sequence of my four children, I would have played peek-a-boo with her and hugged her anyway whether she liked it or not. Instead, I behaved toward her like a girl who's been scolded for being "too forth-putting," another Victorian warning for young ladies considered too bold. I went out of my way not to offend Temple with my touch and games. Wrong! Wrong! Wrong! Temple wasn't a Victorian, she was a baby!

The pain from this young error explains why it matters so much to me today to talk to mothers. In the rush to hear the bizarre details of autism, the world brushes aside the toll it takes on its caregivers and this indifference contributes to the guilt all parents carry.

Another point: Temple was born a little before the big Bettelheim push, and today it occurs to me that it may have been her salvation. After all, what would I have done a few years later, if Temple's doctor had recommended that she be placed under Bettelheim's care? It was one thing to hold out against Dick, but could I have had the nerve to hold out against a doctor? What kind of argument would I have marshalled? Life and its timing—unlike a movie story—can be extraordinarily haphazard, and sometimes that works in your favor.

After all, a movie story is crafted schematically out of back plots and character sketches, assembled into emotional "beats," which are then nailed together into deliberate arcs, to make a dramatic wagon for actors to climb aboard and drive. Along about twenty minutes into the movie comes what's called in scriptland "the first turning point." The wagon gives a lurch, the actors roll about and shove each other, the beats turn into fist fights and the wagon threatens to come apart. But it doesn't. If it did, that would be the end of the movie and you wouldn't get your money's worth. A movie wagon is built to take the actors, and you along with them, all the way to a second turning point, at which point it will give a final lurch and rush to THE END.

But our family life, from September 1949 to August 1962, didn't follow any tidy construction rules. It had its emotional beats all right, but they were confused and I denied them or concealed them or didn't even know what they were. The turning points arrived in misplaced jolts, so there was never anything to do but hang onto the sides of the wagon, careen along as best we could, and in the words of Mrs. Huckle, do our "veddy, veddy best."

In the open question period that follows each lecture—I now lecture often for Future Horizons—experienced parents want to know specific details: how did I deal with this or that problem. But those who've just learned their child is autistic are still too much in shock to ask public questions. They're the ones who seek me out in private, the ones for whom I've learned to take a long time washing my hands in the ladies' room, where invariably one of them slips alongside me.

"Have you got a moment?" she'll ask. There amid the flushing toilets, the roar of the hand dryer, she pours out her grief over the loss of the child she thought she'd bear, the maternal role she thought she'd play out. She reminds me of a photo I once saw of a teenage autistic boy. The camera had caught him, eyes shut, leaning over sniffing at a door latch. His face is contorted into a distressingly grotesque grimace. Over what? Joy in smelling things? Recognition of a familiar latch? His idea of a smile for the camera? All I'm told is that he's making wonderful progress and smelling is the way he identifies things. In the background of the photo, slightly out of focus, his mother watches him. The blur of her anxious face is all there is to her story.

It's the same kind of distress a caregiver must suffer over an Altzeimer patient. The person whom the caregiver has known and loved—who once loved her in return—has disappeared. So a piece of the caregiver has disappeared too. But it's the caregiver who feels the loss.

Often women come up to me with secret questions about God, questions they don't dare ask their pastor, or a parent, or perhaps even their mate. "Do you believe in God?" they whisper, looking frantic and not wanting to be overheard. They've been raised to believe that God loves them, that His eye is on the sparrow.

"Then why isn't His eye on *my* sparrow?" Autism feels to them like a spiritual betrayal.

Occasionally a father will speak to me after a lecture, interesting because autism is a five to one male disorder. Autism is harder for men than for women. Women bring life into the world and on the whole we pretty much accept what comes. Our bodies and our dispositions are built for flexibility. We swell with each pregnancy, then slip back into our old shape. Our breasts fill with milk and empty. We take in what comes and give out what we can. We accept.

Men are built to resist and stand fast, their muscles are hard to the touch, they need physical strength to hold them to their honorable intent. The downside of that honor is shame. One father tells me, "Everything you said your husband went through, I had to go through before I could accept my child."

Another says, "I look at my child and see myself."

A cowboy father with haunted eyes tells me his child's autism is the price of his horse whispering. "I can talk to horses. I know how to train them, I can make a horse do anything. But I can't talk to people. That's why it's my fault my child is autistic."

An Asian father is past explaining. His wife protests, murmuring softly, "We must learn to live without hope." No, he intends to confront me with his question:

"What if we can't stand it?"

I recognize in that moment, that Dick couldn't stand it either. And in exactly the same way. It was too crazy, too dark, too close to his own edgy soul. His shame went underground and turned into rage against me.

As I wrestle with the questions parents ask, I discover that my relationship to them will not be to tell stories or give specific, "how to," advice, but to give them—from the vantage point of years—an overall insight to carry them through the daily strain of raising an autistic child. To do a good job of that, I will have to learn for myself the basic problems of the autism disorder.

What do we mean by contextual thinking and conceptual thinking? What produces mind sidedness? Over systemizing? Obsessive and repetitive behavior patterns? How does a lack of eye contact affect empathy? Ego? Exactly what is the full syndrome of autism?

The full syndrome of autism. That's the ticket. Time to start on that trip up the Nile.

Chapter 9

Looking for the Source

My first look at today's medical research on autism takes me to Pittsburgh to interview Dr. Nancy Minshew, Associate Professor of Psychology and Neurology and head of the Autism Project at the University of Pennsylvania Medical Center.

I find her small and breezy and immediately want to call her "Nancy." She and Joyce Douglas, who's introduced me, are clearly old chums, Joyce having been president for many years of ABOARD, Pittsburgh's parent association for autism. Pittsburgh is a city that functions like a small town; everybody knows each other and gives real credence to Hillary Clinton's line that it takes a village to raise a child.

Dr. Minshew talks hard and fast, racking up her points with a mammoth compilation of research data. Her intensity seems to spring from a determination to change the destiny of Pittsburgh's autistic young. After all, they're the children of her friends.

Her most valuable point, at the heart of her immense research project, is her conviction that there's a biologic bias in most human brains toward understanding things conceptually and this bias is missing in people with autism.

"For example, you could say to an autistic child 'Point to the shovel,' and the child can point to it. But if you say 'Point to the thing you dig with,' they may not know what you're talking about. Whereas a normal toddler, born with the ability to see the world conceptually, may ask before he's even learned what a shovel is called, 'Where's the thing I dig with?'"

"A baby has to begin immediately interpreting things in a meaningful way," Dr. Minshew says, "Because if he didn't, and he looked out on the world, he'd have an awful lot of trouble to survive.... And in autism that's sort of reversed. They get the details, but they don't get the concept.... There's a barrier in the brain-wiring against understanding things conceptually."

When children with autism come into this room, "they see three people, but they also see the pictures on the wall, the furniture, the calendar, the books, and they don't know how to sort it out. They're overrun with details, and their memory for those is really great. They have all the facts and that all the more confuses the meaning. It's part of what gives them the oddity."

Dr. Minshew tells the story of the four-year-old child who, every time he came in to her office, pulled out the same medical book (he knew exactly where it was), turned to the same picture (he knew where that was, too), and asked her the same question. Yet clearly he did not understand the text of the book. When he went home that afternoon, he took the guppies out of the fish bowl and held them in his hand overnight and couldn't understand why they were dead in the morning. "Something other children would understand automatically, something as simple as you don't take the fish out of the water. He did twice. It took him twice to figure it out, and then he lost interest in the fish. He said they were broken."

Since people with autism get the details of what they see, but don't encode them in the way we do, they have to figure out a concept or pattern through logic and consciously-memorized rules. They're good at memory. "That part of their brain works really well. But even when they learn the rules, they don't learn them in enough different ways that they can apply them flexibly. And there are some concepts where there is no rule to figure out. Irony. They just don't get it. That higher order cognitive ability isn't there."

Then there are the very young autistic children: "they don't even get rules. They don't get anything, they don't associate a meaning with anything. They don't have a word that goes with an object. They don't have the concept that there is a word that goes with the object. It's part of the problem."

A major thrust in Dr. Minshew's research is to locate this neural brain glitch. "We don't think about it, but our brain is doing these computations automatically, like a computer. You don't think about what your computer is doing. In fact, you don't even look at your fingers when you are typing on your computer. Your thinking has gone into the areas of the brain where it's no longer conscious."

A computer. Dr. Minshew's words set me to analogous thinking. Like an autistic child, a computer functions only on rules and logic. It, too, has facts and memory, it, too, is unable to process concepts. Like the child holding onto the guppies, the computer doesn't get it, can't get it, is missing that particular wiring. Instead, the little paper clip man pops up on the computer screen with his oddly imperious and vaguely threatening warning.

"You are committing an illegal operation."

I am? What have I done? A stab of guilt runs through me, a terrible anxiety that I've damaged my expensive computer. I turn it off and rush to call a friend. "Did you type in the wrong e-mail address?" the friend asks. Could have. I turn the machine back on. The warning has vanished. The computer makes no apology and has no remorse. Because it cannot encode something that exists only as a concept, it cannot encode the value difference between typing in the wrong e-mail address and bringing a gun through airport security. It simply sees both as an error.

Autistic children have the same mindset. A leaf blowing from a tree can create as much anxiety as a manhole cover blowing off in the street. Without the ability to conceptualize, all reality comes barreling at an autistic child, all equally important. As Dr. Minshew says, "It's as if all the planes landed at O'Hare Airport at the same time."

At the next autism conference Temple and I are both speaking. As I describe Dr. Minshew's research, I can see Temple sitting among the parents writing it all down. From now on she will call conceptual thinking "thinking in categories." Not quite the same thing, but a highly workable substitute for what she's missing.

At last I understand what Temple means when she says she's like Mr. Spock, that she has no subconscious. It's not a subconscious she lacks, but Dr. Minshew's conceptual capacity. Dr. Minshew knows Temple and loves to hear Temple say, "I've got that one figured out."

"She's learned to do just that. Figure it out."

"My mind is a series of videos," Temple announces to her audience. "I scan my videos and pick out the one that answers the problem." It brings to mind a mother who's told me about her autistic son who has trouble falling asleep at night.

"I have all these TV sets," her little boy tells her. "I have to turn them all off before I can sleep." How exhausting to go through every hour of every day consciously registering and recording what you and I take in at a single glance. However, despite exhaustion, he's learning to do it, as Temple learned long ago to categorize.

My next step is to find out how he is learning to do it.

I fly to the University of North Carolina in Chapel Hill to talk to Psychologist Gary Mesibov, Ph.D., researcher on autism and the primary organizer of TEACCH,* a leading therapy technique.

Dr. Mesibov agrees that people with autism lack conceptual thinking, but adds that they also don't see things in context. "There's also what you would call a lack of central coherence."

"If you want to summarize what TEACCH is," Dr. Mesibov explains, "it's taking what we know about the brain and presenting the world at the level that autistic children are able to manage and understand ... and they understand it by a lot of little bits, not by understanding the overall concept."

"Are you telling me that these children literally cannot see the forest for the trees?"

Dr. Mesibov nods. "Your daughter is very connected to that; she's very articulate in describing how she remembers things."

I think of Temple's series of videos. I also recall a class of young children that I'd watched recently at the Watson Institute in Sewickley, Pennsylvania,** where I'd been struck by the variety and ingenuity of its teaching techniques. I call Watson's director, Marilyn Hoyson, Ph.D., for the secret to the TEACCH system success, and she says that its most important element is its use of visuals.

"Individuals with autism are visual learners, so we employ the TEACCH visual technique of using pictures and objects to explain concepts, ask questions and give directions. It's using a strength to help them to learn or understand something new."

Dr. Hoyson then explains that, since no two children are alike, Watson's teachers and therapists also include other research-based strategies, such as the Picture Exchange System (PECS) and Applied Behavior Analysis (ABA). Dr. Hoyson is eloquent on the importance of using a variety of approaches, also on the importance of teamwork.

---

* Treatment & Education of Autistic and Related Communication Handicapped Children. An international, interdisciplinary center for research, service and training in autism. Department of Psychiatry, School of Medicine, University of North Carolina at Chapel Hill.
** Educational organization specializing in the education of children with special needs; also in the education of the professionals and pre-professionals who serve them.

"What you were watching appeared to you to be individual work, but behind each child is a carefully developed team collaboration, a pooling of everybody's insight." Her point brings to mind Dedham Country Day school's teamwork help for Temple when she was little, also Hampshire Country School's teamwork when she was a teenager.

Teaching a child with autism how to do a simple task—pushing a button through a buttonhole or asking for a glass of juice—is not unlike showing him how to put together a Lego figure. His life experience, like a Lego kit, has arrived unassembled, and he has to be shown how to fit each piece of reality onto the next one until the world around him is no longer an unassembled jumble but has taken on a meaningful shape.

For this task, Velcro is indispensable. If a child wants juice, he takes his picture of a glass of juice, sticks it onto his Velcro chart, and brings it to the teacher.

"Oh, you want juice?" the teacher asks. She always speaks the words and, after a bit, the child understands them.

He nods (some autistic children rarely speak).

"Is that all you want?" The child thinks a moment. He'd like crackers to go with his juice. So, now, he must fetch his picture of crackers, stick that onto his Velcro chart beside the juice picture, and bring his Velcro chart back to the teacher.

"Oh, you'd like crackers with your juice?" The child nods. The teacher always makes the child figure out for himself what it is he wants. That's hard for some of these children, whose thinking is entirely visual and memory-driven. There are those who aren't even aware that they want something.

Watching the Watson Institute class in action has brought to mind Temple's nanny teaching Temple long ago how to color pictures: first, pick out the right color to go with the picture; next, keep the crayon within the lines. Only today do I appreciate her gift to Temple and wish she were still alive to enjoy the handiness of Velcro.

Prepositions present another learning hurdle. Since they're not visual objects, prepositions require an autistic child to make a tiny step into the abstract. First, the teacher demonstrates with a set of cars and roads and bridges what she means by "over." (The classroom has a whole play area for this lesson). Then she asks the child, "Can you take the yellow truck and make it go *over* the bridge?"

After he learns to do that, she gives him the next bit of Lego instruction.

"OK, now let's see if you make the blue car go *under* the bridge." As the child gets the hang of what the teacher is asking him to do, he's also learning colors.

"Good! Perfect! How about making the orange bus go *around* the bridge." Slowly, Lego bit by Lego bit, the meaning of prepositions builds up.

Temple often talks about her trouble with prepositions. In the fifties, schools still had air raid drills. Temple says she finally learned "under" by recalling how they all got *under* the school table when the drill bell rang.

Along with "preposition" trouble comes another problem. Though autistic thought is visually-driven, people with autism really don't want to look you in the eye. Eye contact tells them nothing, it only makes them nervous.

Ami Klin Ph.D., head of the Yale Child Study Center in New Haven, Connecticut, has performed eye tracking tests on young people with autism. He found that when they watch a movie, they don't maintain eye contact with the actors on the screen, as do most viewers. Instead their eyes rove about the background, picking up irrelevant details: doorways, pictures on the wall, beads around a girl's neck, etc. Sometimes they watch mouths, which makes sense logically—that's where the words are coming out—but it's not where meaning is.

Dr. Klin's tests have also brought to light the autistic inability to see personality in an animated cartoon of an object. When shown an animation of two little balls chasing each other, the big ball bullying the little ball and shutting it up in a box, people with autism do not see the balls as having personalities nor do they see the box as a lock-up. They see nothing more than two balls and a box. They don't get the gist of the story. They're equally baffled by word stories. Whatever the form, stories and imaginative play are often beyond their reach.

Dr. Klin's clinic works with people with autism, trying to teach them how to recognize eye and face signals: happy, sad, angry, wistful, baffled. He's found that they can learn to recognize broad emotions like "happy" and "angry," but more subtle expressions continue to escape them. I think of Dr. Minshew's observation: "Even when they learn the rules, they don't learn them in enough different ways that they can apply them flexibly. Then there are times when there's no rule to figure out. Irony. They just don't get it."

Nor do people with autism understand a wink, which is, in essence, a shared joke.

Yet, reading eye signals is in all animal life, along with the instinct to frolic. The other day, I watched the family dog, cat, and bird carry on a wildly funny game of "Watch, Spring, and Pounce." The bird, bored with whistling in his cage and nobody paying him any attention, flew out the door of his cage and perched on the lampshade above the cat. The cat was instantly alert. Then the dog got up from his corner to watch the cat. When the bird saw that he had everybody's attention, he swooped across the room. The cat sprang over the furniture after him, and the dog, though he knew he shouldn't, raced after the cat with a clatter of claws. As soon as the bird had them both in a frenzy, he flew back to his post on the lampshade. The cat returned to his sofa pillow, and the dog, with a sigh, settled back into his corner to watch the cat. As soon as they were both quiet, the bird repeated his game. Over and over the three did this, until, finally, satisfied with the mayhem he'd stirred up, the bird flew back to the boredom of his cage.

It was a game based on eye contact, also involving risk, rules, and some kind of agreed upon trust. Yes, the bird ran a risk, but he knew he could fly out of the cat's reach, and clearly the sport of the tease made it worthwhile. The dog, adept at eye contact* and by nature a rule follower, knew he wasn't supposed to chase the cat, but he also knew that, if the cat broke the chase rule, he could break it too. That was the rule. Each animal kept his eye on the other, and, as long as the rules stayed in place, it was just a game. But what about trust? When the bird flew back to his cage, how did the bird know the cat wouldn't scramble up the side of the cage and claw him out the open door, as he'd clawed out the baby chipmunks living in the bird house hanging on the garden tree?

"Because," Temple says "the animal rule is, 'You don't kill where you eat.'" That's a rule she can understand intellectually, but understanding eye signals, which are emotional and ever shifting, still escapes her. Yet without eye signals, how can you develop empathy? Again it's *Star Trek's* Mr. Spock, who can't fathom why humans are so emotional.

Considering these wicked neural bites—concepts, context, eye signals, empathy—it's not surprising that the life of a person with autism may end up being one of self-absorption. This can be a bit of a heartbreak for parents. When autistic children have been taught how to react in an emotionally appropriate way, we tend to assume an empathy that perhaps isn't possible. That's when we get hurt.

---

* "Don't catch the dog's eye," we say, "or he'll come over and beg for attention."

Gertrude Stein was once quoted as saying, "There's no there, there." Exactly who or what she was remarking about I can't vouch for, but when you see how these key lacks limit spontaneous reactions, they're words to keep in mind. Because autistic people can be missing the core sensibility that most of us come equipped with, what we teach them—not only about prepositions and eye contact, but about emotions and face signals—they will accept literally and live by. I agree that, without this "figured out" teaching, an autistic person might be doomed to a life of confusion. Nevertheless, it's important to remember that the empathy we've taught him, is ours. The eye signals are ours. We have imposed our reactions on him and he may lack the emotional ammunition to challenge them. It behooves us, therefore, to be very sure we are giving him our best.

In her younger years, Temple found it hard to clarify the difference between conclusions she'd reached on her own, and those she'd acquired from somebody else. Certain emotions, like her very honest feeling for her squeeze machine, were unmistakably hers. Others, though she presented them as hers, sometimes had a secondhand feel. Yet, given the terms of her autism, how could she know the difference between reactions she'd beachcombed and those that were legitimately hers?

What comes to mind is the long ago incident of Temple's expulsion from high school, when a bunch of school girls called her "retard," and Temple threw a book at one of them. It was years before Temple told me she couldn't read their faces then, can't always read faces today, may perhaps be still missing that particular sliver of life. Back then, she certainly had no way to know whether the girls were her friends or whether she was the target for their ridicule. By the same limitation, if she couldn't read their faces, how could she be sure what her face was supposed to look like in return? Was it a joke? Should she laugh? Or was it that particular brand of female malice? All she could do was lash out blindly.

Then slowly, with no innate concept, no intuitive clue—conscious intelligence her only guide, and even then not sure—she's taught herself over the years to prepare her face "to meet the faces that you meet."

How bright and brave of her to want to meet us anyway, armed with such a flimsy, homemade mask.

As if all this weren't enough for an autistic person to contend with, there's also the challenge of asymmetry. As humans, none of us is evenly balanced. Our face is lopsided, and so is our body. For no apparent reason, our heart is on the left and our stomach on the right. Our brain, too, is lopsided, the left side working for organization, the right in the service of beauty and art.*

My next pursuit is to find out how our lopsidedness affects autism.

In search of an answer, I pay a visit on Eric Hollander, M.D., Professor of Psychiatry and Clinical Director of the Seaver Autism Research Center at Mt. Sinai Hospital in New York City. Tall and friendly, Dr. Hollander ushers me into his sunny office. On the bookshelf behind him, prominently displayed, is the published program supplement of his 2001 Seaver Autism Research Center Symposium with a picture of Temple on the cover. It seems Temple delivered a key lecture that year to an international assembly of doctors. My feelings? Picture a Norman Rockwell illustration of motherly pride.

How would I describe Dr. Hollander? Well, for starters, what intrigues me is the slow measured tone of his voice, in direct contrast to the import of what he's saying. He could be delivering a carefully tallied balance sheet to a board room of bankers. Is it a kind of shyness? Or is it years of hiding his hunches behind the

---

* Canaries sing out of the left side of their trachea.

graphs and charts of acceptable medical fact? Scientists like to present studies they can prove and back up with statistics. They hold a longtime scunner against the word "imagination," preferring the safe pomposity of "conceptual leap." As if "imagination," given its head, might run off in any old flighty direction and meddle with accepted facts. Yet here's Hollander, his measured cadence addressing cutting edge speculations on the lopsided nature of autism and Asperger's.*

"As far as the differences between Asperger's and autism...there are some people who believe that the only difference has to do with speech and language.... Autism with good language functioning is really to look at Asperger's.... There are other individuals who believe that...one is a right brain illness and the other is a left brain illness. Autistic brains evidence a left brained lack and therefore, have developed an excess of right-brained skills. Whereas Asperger's brains evidence a right-brained lack and have developed a left brain excess. Autism and Asperger's may very likely be right-brained and left-brained illnesses."

Dr. Hollander keeps using phrases like "there are those who believe," so I ask him directly does he, himself, believe it? He thinks a moment, then nods. Right away I suspect his careful measured voice to be protective coloring.

"Autistic people have extraordinary visual/spatial skills and ability to integrate visual memory. Whereas Asperger's individuals evidence a right brain deficiency, lots of problems with visual/spatial skills, but advanced verbal and language skills..."

"You know, the thing that really is amazing about individuals in the spectrum, there are real peaks and valleys. Some skills that are really deficient and other skills that are really extraordinary. Temple's a good example, there are these particular areas where she's really extraordinary...Clearly she has extraordinary visual, spatial skills." (On the deficit side, Temple herself will tell you she can't balance on one foot, walk a chalk line, or do algebra.)

---

* "Asperger's," first defined by Dr. Hans Asperger, is a milder form of the autism syndrome.

I ask Dr. Hollander for an official medical definition of autism and Asperger's.

"Autism is a multi-genetic disorder where there is difficulty in three domains: social interaction/social deficit domain, speech and language, narrowness of interest and repetitive behaviors. Asperger's is related to social deficit and behavior domain. Children with Asperger's have normal speech and language, or very often very advanced speech. Whereas autistic individuals often have a deficit."

Today's definition also includes people with milder and varying degrees of autism-related conditions, which has raised the ratio of autism from one in five hundred, to one in two hundred. However, the ratio of males to females remains at five males to one female.

Whether the rise in autism is due to more specific diagnoses, or whether it's actually on the increase, is an open question, and one that concerns doctors deeply.

My interview with Dr. Hollander took place in 2001. Since then, the lopsided aspect of autism have been explored more fully by Simon Baron-Cohen, Ph.D., whom Dr. Hollander presents at his 2003 Symposium. Dr. Baron-Cohen's field of study is Asperger's, where the ratio of males to females jumps up to ten to one. Asperger's people often have exceptional intelligence, but lack a sense of social exchange and empathy. Without help, they can end up as long-winded bores holding forth endlessly (and brilliantly) on their own interests, oblivious to ours. Not so long ago we called them eccentric and avoided them if we could, leaving them bewildered and lonely.

Dr. Baron-Cohen has come forward with a new evaluation of this unhappy phenomenon: the extreme male brain. The left side of the brain is known to be the systemizing side. Dr. Baron-Cohen attributes its over-systemizing, (the big Asperger's problem) not just to a lack of development of the right side, as Dr.

Hollander put forward in 2001, but to an excess of testosterone. (A theory proposed earlier by Hans Asperger.)

"I suggest," Dr. Baron-Cohen writes, "that two neglected dimensions for understanding human sex differences are empathizing, and systemizing. The male brain is defined psychometrically as those individuals in whom systemizing is significantly better than empathizing, and the female brain is defined as the opposite cognitive profile. Using these definitions, autism can be considered as an extreme of the normal male profile.

"… Systemizing is our most powerful way of understanding and predicting the law-governed inanimate universe. Empathizing is our most powerful way of understanding and predicting the social world. Systemizing and empathizing are entirely different kinds of processes…. And ultimately … are likely to depend on independent regions in the human brain."*

Dr. Baron-Cohen backs up his research findings with impressive data, but notes that not all men are systemizers and not all women are empathizers.

Both Dr. Baron-Cohen and Dr. Hollander note that the exaggerated asymmetry of autism and Asperger's usually appear in a milder form in other members of the family.

"Fathers and grandfathers (on both sides of the family) of autistic individuals are over-represented in occupations such as engineering, which requires good systemizing, but in which a mild impairment in empathizing would not necessarily be an impediment to success." Simon Baron-Cohen**

"We've been very interested in the repetitive behavior domain. There are some autistic individuals who have these special interests they get absorbed in … very narrow, restrictive, repetitive interests…and when we look in the family, the parents also have these special repetitive interests … It doesn't mean that the family members have autism. No. What they have is a one-key

---

* New Insights in The Diagnosis, Neurobiology, Genetics and Treatment of Autism. The Mount Sinai School of Medicine Symposium 11/2/03.
** Ibid

symptom domain…" Eric Hollander

Dr. Hollander winds up our interview talking about the value to the human race of temperament and exaggerated traits:

"It helps the survival of the species to have a broad range of different traits … People in the autism spectrum who have extraordinary mathematical, visual, and artistic ability. You need them just as you need people who have extraordinary social abilities, and people who will take great risks and others who can anticipate problems and are risk avoiders. People with bi-polar [manic/depressive] illness can be extremely creative. We also need obsessive-compulsives. You want all these traits in the population. They don't become disorders until they cause marked stress or interfere with functioning in some way."

The research of both men brings to mind Darwin's "survival of the fittest," in that it refers to more than a mere competitive nature "red in tooth and claw." It also means survival of the gene fittest to serve the species.

Taking leave of Dr. Hollander, I depart ruminating on his list of exaggerated human traits, how we rely on them with no thought of the toll they take on human nerve. Actors, particularly comics, are known to be manic depressives, but, whatever the cost to them personally, they never let us see their downside.

And who dreams up those peculiar train schedules: the 11:59, the 8:03? An obsessive does, that's who. And we want him to be obsessive; we're counting on those extra minutes.

At a Salt Lake City conference, I run into an engineer/ computer expert who has an autistic boy. He and his wife have been giving family statistics and, as the man puts it, "gallons of blood" to a huge autism genetic research program at the University of Utah. The engineer and Dr. William McMahon, the project's "principal investigator," have become fast friends. The engineer laughs, "We recognize that we're both obsessive systemizers."

Well, there it is.

The engineer's words, the doctors' words. It all points to what I can no longer put off examining: how the genetic traits on both sides of our family have contributed to Temple's autism.

No, wait. Here's a brief reprieve. Future Horizons has invited me to speak in Anchorage, Alaska, that last bastion of Dr. Hollander's risk takers.

It's May. The winter avalanches are still frozen hard to the mountain gullies and the trees give no sign of sprouting buds. But daylight is already stretching out, putting forth long evenings of blue dusk with a midnight rim of light waiting to turn into dawn. Before you know it the sun is up all over again, throwing its beams in between the low buildings and across the harbor.

Everwhere in Anchorage extremes jostle together: teetotalers and staggering drunks, atheists and Born Again Christians, millionaires in chalets and bums in broken down trailers, boredom and adrenaline-rush emergencies. Most of all, endless sun or endless night.

"How do you explain the darkness to an autistic child," a father asks. "How do you make him understand that the sun won't come up till 10:30 a.m., and will be gone by 3:00 p.m.? We've tried everything, every kind of light you can buy."

I have no answer. Instead I urge hanging onto something that has meaning for you and end up quoting T.S. Eliot.

As I come out of the conference hall a mother yells, "Bingo!" Then seeing that I look surprised, fills me in. "For you it's T.S. Eliot, for me it's Tuesday night Bingo!"

We have lunch in the lobby of the conference hall where the walls, carpet, and stairs have been done in pale summer blossoms of Inuit color, lime, brick, blue, aqua, and orange.

A mother wants me to advise her on her eighteen-year-old twin Asperger boys. "My boys don't like any kind of doubt in their life," she says. "They want everything regimented. All problems must have black and white answers. They long to go into the army, they love the army routine and the army wants them. They've passed all the tests, but I feel so troubled. Should I tell the army doctor that they're Asperger? Would the army doctor care?" I don't have an answer.

Another mother comes up to me, starts out, "It was when you talked about character—" She can get no further, flings herself into my arms and sobs. Again I have no answer.

After the conference a mother drives me along the narrow two-lane highway between the mountains with their ice gullies and the frozen tidal flats. She tells me how the town's people will plant the highway median strip.

"One of these days soon, we'll all turn out for it. We'll clear away the winter debris and plant the whole length of highway with flowers. I wish you could see it, flowers love our Alaskan summers."

She points out the tidal flats. "Those flats are deceptively dangerous. It looks like you could walk on them over to that other mountain, but don't try it. The mud will suck you in up to your knees and unless the rescue team gets to you before the tide comes in, you'll drown. The rescue team has a water pump that forces water into the mud under your feet, it gives you a little man-made tide that lifts you out. Don't ever think you can beat the mud. In winter the avalanches shoot down, cover the highway and bury your car. I never let my kids drive without a cell phone and a flare in case they get caught."

The local bar and grill is Humpy's, named for the humpback halibut they catch in Anchorage, cut in chunks and plunge into a deep fry. Delicious beyond words. Humpy's is a dead ringer for the TV show *Northern Exposure*, complete to bar stools that don't match and mix match customers.

"You're from New York?" they exclaim in cordial amazement. "Hey, the drinks are on us!" Humpy's calls where we come from the "Lower Forty-Eight."

I listen to their yarns, their risky adventures, and think of the 1862 Homestead Act which declared that any United States citizen who was head of a family or twenty-one years of age might apply for a hundred and sixty acres of unappropriated public land and might acquire title to it by living there and cultivating it for five years. Right up to the Act's end in the 1950s, families and companies were still gambling on it here in Alaska.

The Homestead Act also put me in mind of the 1875 adventures of the original Grandin brothers (Dick's grandfather and great uncle) in the North Dakota Red River Valley territory. North Dakota must have been as cold and remote as the Klondike when those two brothers took Horace Greeley's advice to heart, set out for the west, and ended up organizing the biggest wheat farm in the world.

What wonderful family traits those two brothers have handed down to Temple and her siblings. The thought of them is just what I need to send me on the last lap of my journey: a genetic look at both sides of the family.

Chapter 10

The Legacy of Genes

John Livingston Grandin, Dick's grandfather and Temple's great grandfather, and his brother, William James Grandin, were French Huguenots conducting oil drilling operations in Tidioute, Pennsylvania in 1860. Oil paid off handsomely but not as handsomely as it might have. According to family legend, Dick's grandfather was about to negotiate a deal with old man Rockefeller and had set up an appointment to meet him. Rockefeller kept him waiting and Dick's grandfather lost his temper, a trait already apparent in the Grandin men. Refusing to wait longer, he walked out before Rockefeller arrived, thus forfeiting a chance to be in on the ground floor with Standard Oil, a loss the Grandins have lamented ever since.

However, along with the temper came an unerring Grandin talent for organizing existing systems: leasing and subleasing farms, conducting drilling operations, buying and selling crude oil, and building pipelines.

Along with the systemizing came another gift, perhaps even more valuable: a canny eye for potential.

"… In 1868, John L. Grandin and A. Clark Baum established a general banking business … Two years later William J. [Grandin] purchased Baum's interest and the institution became the Grandin Bros. Bank. The Grandin Bank, founded on oil money, was famed from coast to coast for its solvency; it helped Jay Cooke when he financed the Civil War. [There must have been money transactions before the bank was formally set up.] When the Cooke firm went broke in 1873, the Grandins obtained the collateral security on their loans: thousands of acres of undeveloped land in North Dakota. Jay Cooke's share of financing western railroads....*

"... John L. Grandin was a good trader and, rather than take fifteen cents on the dollar, decided in 1875 ... to go west and inspect the Red River Valley of North Dakota."

Noting "the thick deposit of clay sub-soil and two to three feet of dark rich surface soil," he figured it would make good wheat land.

Family lore has it that neither Grandin brother knew much about farming. However, they were quick to see that, although the local farmers owned their own farm equipment, they didn't know how to organize themselves into larger, more effective working systems. The Grandins, good at systems, measured off their acreage in terms of wagon wheel revolutions and figured out the precise amount of seed it would take to plant the entire tract of land with wheat. They then determined how many workers, mules, carts, etc., they would need to plow the acreage, plant the seed, raise the crop and harvest it. Next, they built dormitories to house the workers and their families, figured out the cost of maintaining the dormitories and feeding everybody. They fed them well, as the carefully kept records attest. Anticipating the transportation of the wheat, they looked to the river and bought up river frontage.

"The Grandin brothers constructed and operated a line of river steamers to transport grain and supplies for their farm. This unique aspect of bonanza farming was possible because the

---

* *The Grandin Brothers*, Grandin, North Dakota Centennial Publication, 1881-1981. Associated Printers, Grafton, ND.

Grandins possessed four miles of frontage on the Red River, which enabled them to transport their wheat by river to Fargo, the nearest railroad center ... where the Grandins owned a 50,000 bushel elevator, for transshipment to the railroad ... tying the state and the Northwest to the twin cities of Minneapolis and St. Paul."*

The Grandin systemizing talent put into effect the first undertaking of its kind: a corporate farm.

Young America was booming. An up-and-coming lumber company wanted to buy some of the Grandin land. According to family lore, the brothers again took a look at the land potential and figured that payment in lumber company stock would end up being worth more than ready cash. Once again, their vision paid off. The lumber company turned out to be Weyerhouser.

Now seriously rich, the next generation Grandins returned east and decided to move from Tidioute, Pennsylvania to a big city where they could enjoy a grander lifestyle. They chose Boston, bought a house—first on Commonwealth Avenue and then on the Fenway—but never quite plumbed Boston as the brothers had envisioned North Dakota wheat. Neither Brahmins nor Blue Stockings, they adhered rigidly to what they perceived as the new "society" system, with no insight into Boston eccentricity: the Boston whim of picking and choosing friends with little regard for a rank it no longer cared to feature since it had possessed it for so many generations. Despite their lack of insight, the Grandins accomplished their goal. However, unlike old Boston, they continued to guard their position. No mocking attitudes, no stepping out of line, and no love affairs with impoverished artists. Those were the rules.

All this had been silently drilled into Dick. He had seen his father take a stand against his older sister whose heart was in the arts. Though she was actively discouraged from painting watercolors, she painted them anyway, arranging with a gallery to

---

* Hiram M. Drache, *The Day of the Bonanza, A History of Bonanza Farming in the Red River Valley of the North.* Concordia College, Interstate Printers & Publishers Inc., Danville, Illinois.

exhibit her work. Her father, fearful she might sully the family's social standing, bought up all the paintings before the gallery opening. Dick's sister was then discouraged from marrying the sweet, arty, moneyless man she loved. Instead, she was urged to marry a social scoundrel from Newport who beat her up and stole her jewelry.

Through it all and through the rest of her life, his sister maintained her love of the arts, her dignity, and her genuine gift for friendship. Old Boston adored her. Her father could never figure out why.

One summer day on the Vineyard, her father (Dick's father and Temple's grandfather) brought me a poem he'd cut out of a Northfield School bulletin. He was on the board of the Northfield School and the poem, written by one of its students, had won a big poetry contest. He was proud for Northfield but wasn't sure he understood the poem.

"It's about empathy," I said. "The girl writing the poem is asking the boy to understand her feelings."

"But part of it is in French?"

"That's because she is quoting a line from an old French nursery rhyme, *Au Claire de la Lune.* She's asking the boy to open the door of his heart to her. But, then, to her sorrow, she sees that he's not able to do it. Sometimes people don't know how to open up to each other."

Old Mr. Grandin sighed. He still wasn't sure he understood the poem, but he thanked me for explaining it.

I think of my own parents. Beyond their mundane domestic

exchanges over national politics and neighborhood behavior, I'm not sure that either had much insight into the other, certainly not into each other's dreams.

During the thirties, my father, John Coleman Purves, and three other men invented an electrical coil that could sense direction through the earth's magnetic north. The four men named it the "flux valve" because it registered the minute fluctuations in the earth's force. Later, the Army Air Corps called it "the automatic pilot" and flew their World War II planes by it. After World War II, it took us all the way to the moon. When I look up at the moon, I think of my father, his quiet pride that his flux valve compass walks its bleak dust, registering the pull of our earth.

I wish I knew more about my father, whose documents are preserved in the Smithsonian Museum. How did he meet the three men he worked with? And when? And where? And who did what in those ten years, from 1932 to 1942, when we lived in Springfield, Massachusetts?

First of my father's partners was Haig Antranikian, a small, sallow, sad-eyed Armenian, educated at the University of Cairo.

"Antranikian had the concept," Father said, "but he didn't know what to do with it. I saw how to make it work." Note the word "saw." The family visualizing gene was already in place. My father was both a civil and mechanical engineer, a graduate of M.I.T. and, according to one of his classmates, the brightest man in his class. But my father always said his gift was interpretive, not creative. Father brought in two other men as partners and established The Purves Corporation. The four men then set about to build a working model of Antranikian's idea.

The first of the new partners was Ritchie Marindin, a Frenchman crippled with polio. Though his frame was slight, his shoulders had grown immense from years of swinging his legs between two wooden crutches that squeaked. The other new partner, Lenox F. Beach, was a dour Scot with a bristly sandy mustache, a tall thin man who marched in the Springfield Memorial Day parade in full Scottish regalia beating on the biggest bass drum I've yet to see or hear. He would never look directly at my father's two little girls who watched him goggle-eyed as he marched past us, but his head would give an extra swagger and his arms a wider flourish as he whacked his drum with the huge padded drumsticks.

All through the Depression the four men tinkered away in a second story loft space of the barn housing the Springfield trolley cars. I remember the weeks when they couldn't figure out why their gadget wouldn't hold true, until it dawned on them that it was picking up electric current from the trolley cars parked underneath. Today when I'm in a plane and the pilot landing us asks all passengers to turn off their computers and cell phones, I think of my father and those trolley cars in Springfield.

Most of all, I remember the day when the flux valve compass flew an airborne plane from New York to Chicago with no one touching the controls. The call came through from a friend in New York. I see my father now on the old wall telephone in the back hall, his voice loud because it was long distance and that meant something important. And loud because he was excited. Father was not an excitable man, but he was that day.

Alas, Father's gift and those of his new partners did not include business. It was still the depression. The men had devoted fifteen years to the flux valve and earned nothing; Father so longed for recognition that it rendered him guileless; he rented the Purves Corporation flux valve for a year to Bendix Aviation for $300. At the end of the year he got a another call from New York, from the same friend who'd called him about the flight.

"Jack, I've just heard a Bendix man boast at a cocktail party about their new gadget called a "flux gate." You better get down here. I think they've copied your compass."

They'd copied it all right. They'd turned their $300 rental into a profitable study on how to get round the patents. By now it was World War II, lawsuits were unpatriotic. Bendix put their "flux gate" copy into every American plane.

When the war was over, Sperry Company signed a legitimate contract with my father and built the flux valve into the instrument that took us into outer space. Though the four men finally came into a little money, the government managed to tax them retroactively. How and why I have no idea. Perhaps taxation favors the powerful; perhaps because my father lacked the ability to read the motives of the men with whom he was dealing.

By this time, Antranikian had disappeared. Father went searching for him in New York to give him his share of the profits, eventually locating him in a flophouse on the Bowery. The landlady said the police had carted him off to Bellevue. And there at last Father finally found him.

"I didn't know how to reach you," Antranikian said. "They wouldn't give me paper and pen to write. They asked me what I did for a living. I said I was an inventor, and they laughed at me."

My father told the doctors that Antranikian really was an inventor, got him released from Bellevue, and established him somewhere in the outskirts of Manhattan. After that, he and Father worked for a while developing a system for color television, but the fire had gone out of both of them and another system was put into play.

My father seems to have accepted Antranikian's emotional breakdown without excitement, certainly not with the excitement he would have brought to an engineering problem. Did he ever ask Antranikian what had happened? Was Antranikian able to explain? The two men had known each other for more than twenty years. Was their friendship limited only to theory? Since then, it's crossed my mind that Antranikian may well have been Asperger's, that form of autism that produces mathematical genius coupled with an inability to function socially with the rest of the world.

My father didn't have much of a social compass either. Cerebral, systemizing and reticent, he allowed my mother to impose her social code on his life. His only comment on Antranikian's mental state was to say that it's dangerous to keep theory too much to oneself.

"If you don't have a cohort following the line of logic in your theoretical ideas, pretty soon nobody understands what you're talking about."

That could be, but it could also be that these two complicated men understood each other in the way that today's engineers and computer nerds understand each other and are drawn together through mutual work. Father was more stable than Andronikian; he had a wife and family to tie him to reality.

I asked Father once why he and his partners had persisted with the flux valve for fifteen years against Sperry Company's advice to desist. The head of Sperry was a personal friend of Father's and, from time to time, would ask him, "Why do you keep puttering around with an electric coil? Everybody knows compasses work with needles."

"Why did you?" I asked.

"Because I knew I was right."

He was right, of course, and the flux valve ultimately changed the course of aeronautics. But it must have taken fantastic conviction to keep working on a gizmo that all the engineers at Sperry thought was absurd. Father had an answer to that.

"No original concept ever comes out of company men in a company lab. Those men are joiners; they'd rather be around men who think the same way they do. Given those terms, a company lab can only perfect what has already been conceived and pretty much developed. Original ideas and early development come out of loners—some man tinkering around by himself in a back shed and beating his wife."

I don't know where Father dreamed up "wife beating," unless he was thinking about somebody he knew.

Father taught me calculus and solid geometry, but he was mostly theoretical with me, rarely personal. I like theory. I tend to spin off into it myself, but it must have been very lonely for my mother who hadn't a theoretical bone in her body. Father's answer to her when she took exception to his small social obstinacies was to say, "If it hadn't been the right thing to do, I wouldn't have done it." An answer that enraged her.

My mother's focus was social. She thought she'd married a handsome, suitable Philadelphian who would enhance her social life, never understanding that my father, who adored her, couldn't possibly play out that role. I see her as she was in the thirties, young, pretty, and vivacious, flinging her arms around my father and asking him in a coy, joky way, "Poppa love Mama?" My father would draw away from her as if batting off gnats, "Yes, yes. Poppa love Mama." And yet, when they both were in their seventies, and my mother was hospitalized with a small cancer, my father returned home after the operation and burst into tears.

"She looked so young."

The habit of doing without casual affection became so engrained in my mother that, in later years, she didn't want to be touched at all. I would try to embrace her, but she could only wait stiffly for me to let go. After a while, I stopped trying. My father embraced me only once, but it was heartfelt. I told him I was getting divorced; he put his arms around me and said, "Be brave."

My mother minded the long talks I had with Father. I think because she wasn't interested in what we were talking about and therefore felt excluded. From the time I was little, I had learned that the only way to get my father to talk to me was to ask him questions. His long habit of answering me and explaining made it easier for him in later life to tell me his ideas.

"Mutual attraction," he would say, "lies at the heart of everything. Originality is mental energy focussed, long and obsessively on one, all-consuming goal. Thus focussed, it will attract the answer to it." He thought for a moment, then added, "Newton not only saw the apple fall to the ground, he also saw the ground leap up to meet it." In a corollary to this, he felt that the same new idea, the same new way of perceiving reality, would emerge in different parts of the world at the same time.

"In the thirties, there were other men in other countries fooling around with electric coils."

This mutual attraction of ideas was Father's explanation of luck, but his explanation didn't include the human phenomenon of mutual spiritual attraction. As passionately as nature abhors a vacuum, most of us rush toward each other, mind, body, and heart, in what Lewis Thomas has called the bewildering and "pervasive latency of love." That response was missing in Father.

Today's statistics show that autism runs high among Silicon Valley nerds and in the families of engineers, where it tends to skip a generation, turning up in a grandchild. Father was very proud of Temple, her power of visualization. Perhaps, too, he sensed a kinship with her lacks.

When my father died he'd finished his battle with cancer and was ready to accept death. During his last weeks he lay waiting, stretched out on a wicker sofa, on the porch, his arms crossed on his chest like a crusader. When I woke him to say that I'd be back the following week, he opened one eye and smiled. His eye had the glazed look of a migrating bird dropped from the sky. Sometimes I could revive such birds with a drink of water from a saucer; sometimes the journey had been too much for them and they would look at me with the same glazed eye.

Then Father rallied, so I was ready to deny that look. In his last week at the hospital, the rallying and sinking rose and fell as he struggled each day with finality, and typical of Father, said nothing about it. Instead, he took an innocent pleasure in the hospital nurses, saying, "I've been powdered and petted by more pretty women."

He was particularly fond of one nurse and she of him. She liked to ask him questions.

"Can you imagine?" she said to me, quite delighted. "While I'm helping him struggle to get up from the toilet, he's explaining to me why the Nile runs north!"

How like Father to have found somebody in his last days who would ask him questions and he could explain.

The day before he died, he saw my children and was unbelievably sweet to them, his smile a blessing. The day was so peaceful, so resolved, that I deluded myself into thinking we would have him with us a little longer. The real resolution was Father's.

The next day he waited for my mother and me, as he had waited for "Mary, dear lamb" so many times in his life. Though he was no longer conscious, I felt his concentration. With each hardly discernable breath, he gathered up from deep within himself that universal creative energy he so ardently believed in. Supremely dignified, his equation ready, he slid slowly from his skin, first his feet, then along his torso, his heart, his neck, till the last breath escaped, leaving his mouth open like a hatched egg. The room was full of spirit. I know his equation was received.

At ninety-eight, after suffering a small stroke, my mother, who outlived my father by sixteen years, was still putting off dying in a girlish hope that her life story might yet shift in her favor. But it didn't, and finally, within weeks of death, she said to me, somewhat to her surprise: "I've lived a life of privilege and I've been unhappy most of my life."

What she felt in her final moments I don't know. The nursing home said she died in her sleep. I had wanted so much to be with her, but I wasn't, and she died alone as she felt she had been most of her life. She always said that the tragedy of old age was not that one felt old but that one felt young. A paraphrase she took from Oscar Wilde, without understanding how it revealed her aching disappointment.

A few nights after her death, I dreamed my mother came to me to tell me not to worry about her, that everything was all right now she understood. What she understood or whether the dream was just my own soul trying to garner comfort, I'm not sure. I only know that in life she gave me her love of poetry and her belief in ghosts.

Before my mother died, I told her about the ghost in the Bronxville house. She nodded, "Ah, the smell of cigar smoke."

With that small vote of confidence, though she hated my pop singing, I decided to write John Damon's ghost into a cabaret number and to enlarge it with a song I'd make up called "Briar Rose." The song turned out to be a Victorian lament for lost love, but, since I couldn't forget the feeling of the laughter that had always come with the presence, I gave John Damon a girl named Rose and said that he used to tease her with the song. Gordon Munford, my accompanist, and I worked on the number, but we were both anxious about it. It was so far off of the usual pattern. One night we decided to risk performing it anyway, just to see what would happen.

As the story and song unfolded, the club fell still. No tinkling ice, no murmur of voices. Totally still. When we came to the end, the place went wild, the cabaret equivalent of stopping the show.

As people got up from the bar and began hugging us, Gordon said, "You have to tell them it's your own ghost. Tell them that bit about your son."

At that time, my son owned a blue Nova he loved as only a cowboy loves his horse. He was always tinkering with it, to give it an extra bit of oomph. One day he had it up on cinder blocks and was crawling under it, jazzing it up to do his bidding. It was dusk. I was sitting in the courtyard finishing up the "Briar Rose" song when I heard the sound of his auto jack. I came round to the driveway to see him trying to raise the Nova up even higher. His white shirt was all that showed in the blue twilight.

"I wish you wouldn't work on the car now," I begged. "It's too dark to see anymore."

My son instead of saying "Oh, Mom," said, "Yeh. Maybe you're right."

I realized at once that's why John Damon's presence had always manifested itself at twilight. Blue dusk was the hour when he'd been crushed to death, when it was too dark for him to see what he was doing.

Somehow the ghost, the story, the song, the performance—it was all a gift from my mother.

As was her acting talent.

When I was a child, I watched my mother perform in amateur productions. I found her thrilling, and named my first child "Mary Temple" after her. It's the name my grandmother had given my mother, in memory of her own dead sister, the Mary Temple of Jamesian note. Whether Henry James knew my grandmother or even took notice of her is a moot question. She was still a little girl, sitting with her hands folded in her lap at her uncle's dining table. But James certainly was aware of my grandmother's sister. Known to him as "Minnie Temple," she became the model for Isabel Archer, his heroine in *The Portrait of a Lady*.*

My grandmother and her sister used to stay with their aunt and uncle, the Tweedys, in Newport, Rhode Island. Mr. Tweedy

---

* The name "Mary Temple" decorates various branches of our family tree, so there could be another Mary Temple laying claim to Henry James' "Minnie Temple." If so, now's the moment to step forward.

thought little of "the James boys," as he called them, declaring them "rude and conceited and always late to lunch."

Temple likes to conceal the "Mary" part of her name, preferring the androgyny of "Temple," but it was only by chance that she wasn't called "Mary" for life. One of the Irish girls working for us was named Mary, so to keep the family cast of characters straight, there was "Mary" and "Mary Temple."

"Mary Temple" soon shortened into "Temple."

Temple likes to think of herself as an anthropologist on Mars, but, in truth, she's very much part of the family tradition on this planet. Her concern for the well-being of cattle follows our generational commitment to those less fortunate. My mother's grandmother, Clara Temple Leonard (the mother of Henry James' "Mary Temple") was one of a group of nineteenth century American women who dedicated their lives to improving the lot of the poor, achieving lasting changes in our welfare system.

Clara Temple Leonard was also the first woman in this country, perhaps on this planet, to be proved legally a "person." In 1883, she served in the Massachusetts legislature on the State Board of Health, Lunacy, and Charity, a name mercifully shortened later to the Board of Health. The governor, seeking to replace her and expand his control base with one of his own men, demanded that she be removed from the board on the grounds that a woman was not legally a "person."

Oliver Wendell Holmes Jr., already a judge, declared that, under civil law, a woman is *not* a "person." However, since she's accountable for her actions, under criminal law a woman *is* a "person." The Board of Health, Lunacy, and Charity, as a state board, comes under criminal law. Ergo, Clara Leonard is a person. Though Holmes' legal argument was shaky to the point of absurdity, Clara Temple Leonard accomplished, in her time, a major step forward for women's rights.

Temple, in her time, has achieved a major step forward for the rights of animals. Like her great great grandmother she, too, has a bold and altruistic streak.

As to the Grandin systemizing gene, I'm happy to report that it's alive and well and living in Temple's brother, a fourth generation banker and senior vice president of a distinguished New York bank.

Temple's visualizing ability may have been enhanced by autism, but, basically, it's a family gift, as is evidenced in the decorative wall paintings created by one of her sisters, and in the sculpture created by the other.

And me? Well, I used to think I was different from the rest of the family until I read my father's carefully compiled genealogy. No, I'm not different. I'm just one more in a long line of preachers, teachers, and non-joiners. The renegade trait has been around for generations.

Traits are gifts. Dr. Hollander is right in noting that they survive because the human species needs them. Nevertheless, upon occasion they can combine and produce too much of a good thing, and that in essence, is what autism is: an exaggeration of the family traits. In our family, they're splendid traits, with a splendid history.

All this character evidence should be enough to persuade Temple to let go of her notion about Mars, and lay claim to her earthly genes, which have been handed down to her as lovingly as her name.

Chapter 11

What It Means to Be Human

My last job with the Poets Theatre was in the seventies, as part of an international convention of Jungian psychoanalysts. Harboring a certain anxiety about the nature of their work, wanting to go back to the origins of Jung's thinking, analysts from America and Zurich had gathered in Vezia for a summer of lectures and demonstrations on the various disciplines drawn upon by Jung. It included Jung's own studies, the novels of Hermann Hesse (a follower of Jung), tai chi, and the mythology studies of Joseph Campbell (then still relatively unknown). Since the analysts were also interested in understanding how actors come by their insight into character, a group of us from the Poets Theatre had been brought to Switzerland to perform for them in a series of theatrical readings, culminating in a full performance of Archibald MacLeish's *Herakles*.

Herakles, a lesser-known MacLeish play, deals with the hubris of politics and, to me, it is a more powerful work than *J.B.*, which made a big Broadway splash. It's the story of our own economic and scientific arrogance, reimagined through the old Greek myth of Herakles (Herakles is the Greek name for Hercules). Herakles, if you remember, asked the Delphic Oracle to tell him his destiny. The Oracle told him that, first, he must perform those well-known "seven labors."

After performing the labors, Herakles, full of himself, returns to the Oracle to learn what glorious future lies in store for him. The Oracle refuses to answer, and in a rage, he tears her down from her three cornered perch shouting:

> *By God, I'll give the oracles myself*
> *I'll say and say and say and say,*
> *I'll answer it!*

For this the gods punish him. Unwittingly, Herakles kills his own sons.

It's a powerful play, one that a nation suffering from hubris should pay attention to, before making the decision to "say and say and say and say." The Jungian analysts are moved to wonder about the hubris of their own discipline.

Looking back on that 1973 summer in Switzerland and the analysts who were beginning to question their own techniques, recalling the 1962 doubts that psychiatrists were experiencing over their assessment of autism, I reread Erik Erikson's book, *Insight and Responsibility*.

Erikson published the book in 1964, and the next year came to Harvard, where his acclaim was so great that every undergraduate was clamoring to enroll in his course. In order to winnow out the excess, we undergraduate clamorers were each asked to write a short essay on why we thought we deserved to have the academic rope lifted for us. I don't remember who passed judgment, only that I was allowed in.

Insight and Responsibility was required reading, but in 1965 1 didn't take note of what Erikson was acknowledging in it. However, on rereading the book in terms of what I now know about autism, I spot a cautious shift away from his 1950 loyalty to Freud, expressed in *Childhood and Society*.

Somewhere between 1950 and 1964 (the years of my greatest difficulties with Temple and her father) Erikson had responded to a shrewd dig from the poet W.H. Auden.* Auden had noted in a review, ("Greatness Finding Itself," Mid century, No. 13, June 1960), that psychoanalysts found it difficult to differentiate between action that affects others and private behavior that can be studied in clinical isolation. After puzzling through the interpretive tangle psychiatry had created over "deeds" versus "behaviour," Erikson admits in *Insight and Responsibility* to the "Cartesian straight jacket we [psychoanalysts] have imposed on our model of man."** Somewhere in this murky period, was the psychoanalytic world readying itself for major interpretive changes? If so, what's startling is that it took so long, that Descartes' concept of human thought as a little "homunculus" sitting up in our brain telling us what to do, persisted unchallenged for three hundred years. Not only persisted, but directly influenced the psychoanalytic notion that talk alone could unravel emotional disorder, even such a protean one as autism.

When did the psychiatric world release autism from its psychosocial shackles and turn it over to the bioneurologists? And why, despite the 1964 research linking autism to epilepsy, did it take until 1985 for the neurological information to reach the family pediatricians who were examining autistic children and advising desperate parents?

According to Gary Mesibov, Ph.D., psychiatry never gave any public explanation for this diagnostic change-over. Though Leo Kanner regretted his remark about refrigerator mothers, psychiatrists, as a group, didn't acknowledge the shift, nor did they apologize for the pain they'd caused. Instead, they stepped quietly aside, allowing the term "infant schizophrenia" to fade discreetly away.

We mothers would have liked an apology. We deserve it. And

---

* Erik Erikson, *Insight and Responsibility* Norton, New York 1964, pp.162-165.
** Referring to Descartes and his school of philosophy, 1637.

so do the fathers. Today in Europe there are still anguished parents who are being led to believe in Bettelheim. Here in the States, what with books and magazine articles, he's out of the picture, but that isn't good enough. Even today, mothers in this country tell me their distress over pediatric ignorance and callousness.

"I was sent home with very little help and more questions."

"He just went 'Oh.' He treated me like ... he brushed me off."

I was lucky. I look back at my first meeting with Dr. Caruthers and realize how carefully vague both he and Dr. Meyer were in their first diagnosis of Temple, Dr. Meyer simply calling Temple "a very odd little girl." Perhaps both she and Dr. Caruthers sensed that I was young and naive. What would be gained by frightening me with an alarming label? Dr. Meyer was European; she might have believed in Bettelheim, but if so, she kept it to herself. Dr. Caruthers was a kindhearted old Yankee with progressive ideas. He recommended that Temple have an EEG to test for retardation, also to see if she had petit mal, a mild form of epilepsy. The autism/epilepsy connection wouldn't be a known fact for another fifteen years, which in my books, puts Dr. Caruthers neurologically way ahead of his time.

It will take another time lapse before researchers begin to scale the neural complexities of human consciousness: exactly what is it that holds our five senses to a consistently relevant response? Where and how, in each passing moment, do nerves, emotion, and intellect intersect?

V. S. Ramachandran, M.D., Ph.D., in his book, *Phantoms in the Brain,** explores what he calls the "internal construct" responsible for ordering "life's chaos into a stable and internally consistent belief system." By way of a lead-in, he discourses on "qualia," an ancient philosopher's term for "subjective sensation." Dr. Ramachandran uses a color blind scientist to illustrate qualia, a scientist who understands the physical laws of color and

* *Phantoms in the Brain*, Ramachandran & Blakeslee, Quill, William Morrow, New York, 1998.

wavelength processing but cannot actually "see" the color red.

Qualia are "aspects of my brain state that seem to make the scientific description [of red] incomplete—from my point of view."

According to Dr. Ramachandran, once a qualis laden perception has been created, the brain is stuck with it. A good example is the familiar puzzle picture of a dalmation dog.

At first, the picture is all in fragments.*

"Then suddenly everything clicks and you see the dog. The next time there's no way you can avoid seeing the dog. Indeed we

---

* Illustration by Dean Gardei, (c) Intelligence Amplification, Inc. Used with permission.

have recently shown that neurons in the brain have permanently altered their connections once you have seen the dog...."

The dalmatian picture may possibly throw light on one physical aspect of autistic consciousness. Somehow, the neurons in an autistic brain don't appear to alter their connections in the same way as they alter for the rest of us. Yet here is what's curious. If a person with autism can see the dalmation—and he may be able to, autistic people are good at figuring out puzzle faces incorporated into a landscape picture—he can see it just as easily upside down as right side up. Whereas you and I, if we turn the picture upside down, we can no longer construct the dalmation, even though our brain has already registered it, right side up. For us, the picture has lost its visual relevance—*from our point of view.*

What about emotional relevance?

With this quest in mind, I attend a lecture at the 92nd Street Y in New York City, given by behavioral neurologist Antonio Damasio, Ph.D. He has been presenting his studies on the nature of consciousness in a series of books beginning with *Descartes' Error.** At this lecture, Dr. Damasio tells us that we're not thinking beings who feel, but feeling beings who think. In other words, the body informs the mind, not the other way around, as Descartes thought back in 1637.

Somehow, we've always known this. Despite Descartes' faith in his "homunculus," that little man sitting up in our brain telling us what to feel, we've always had a "gut" sense that something more than mere mental activity was producing our emotional take on life. "I feel it in my bones," we say. Or "My heart sank." Clear, everyday human hunches that more is going on somewhere else.

"Feelings point us in the proper direction, where we may put the instruments of logic to good use... They are the result of a most curious physiological arrangement that has turned the brain into the body's captive audience."

---

* Antonio Damasio, *Descartes' Error*, Avon Books Inc., NY. 1994.

Dr. Damasio calls the entire process "the feeling brain."

During the lecture question period, someone in the audience asks him, "Is there free will?"

He allows that there is "but not as much as we wish there were."

Dr. Damasio opens his book, *Descartes' Error,** an exploration of the neurological connections between feeling and decision-making, with the hundred and fifty-year-old tale of Phineas Gage. In essence, it's a nineteenth century story of a man whose skull was shot through by a tamping iron. Amazingly, Gage survived the accident, but his judgment and character were irrevocably changed. Today, Gage's skull, which resides in the Warren Medical Museum of the Harvard Medical School, has been subjected to innumerable MRI's and image scans. Though the scans show no destruction of the areas for motor function and language, Gage's physical brain loss produced emotional and social lacks surprisingly similar to those evidenced by Dr. Damasio's patients suffering from brain tumors in the same neural region. They are also similar to those experienced by people with autism.

Temple, in her own book** makes an insightful observation on this:

> *According to Antonio Damasio, people who suddenly lose emotions because of strokes often make disastrous financial and social decisions. These patients have completely normal thoughts, and they respond normally when asked about hypothetical social situations. But their performance plummets when they have to make rapid decisions without emotional cues. It must be like suddenly becoming autistic. I can handle situations where stroke patients may fail because I never relied on emotional cues in the first place. At age forty-seven, [now fifty-seven], I have a vast databank, but it has taken me years to build up my library of experiences and learn how to behave in an appropriate manner.****

I read Temple's words and think of her struggle to deal with life, equipped only with logic and memory, her "gut" feelings too irrelevant to count on. I read Dr. Damasio's statement, "Our minds would not be the way they are if it were not for the interplay of body and brain during evolution, during individual development and at the current moment."

If Dr. Damasio is right, if human consciousness is composed of a series of interrelated neural procedures woven into the entire body system and our appraisal of it depends upon our "feeling history," what does that suggest about Temple's infant development when "feeling" first began to register on her? If from the hour she was born, Temple found all human touch alarming, how did that alarm emotion affect the neural growth of her feeling response?

If her only escape from alarm was in sleep, did oversleeping rob her of the stimuli she needed for the development and interconnection of the neural circuits that would in time become her feeling brain?

I was young and ignorant. I misread oversleeping as "a good baby." It never occurred to me, nor might it occur to a mother today, to wake up an oversleeping baby.

Nevertheless, if you ask Temple today if she wants her autism "cured," she says no. No matter how difficult her struggle for what we interpret as relevant, she wants to hold onto her feeling history as she sees it *from her point of view.*

Unable to let go of these thoughts, I now brood on the feeling history of Temple's siblings. Little has been said at conferences about the toll autism takes on siblings: the playground humiliations, the spoiled friendships, the invasion of their small play space at home. I think of my long-ago inability to explain Temple's autism to the siblings, who were younger than Temple and often bewildered by her behavior. At the time, my own struggles seemed to be all I could handle, or thought I could handle, with the result that I told them nothing. I expected them to have an adult's intuition and somehow, they managed to achieve just that. But it was asking too much of them and today, it troubles me. What about their feeling history?

Today, in Salt Lake City, Nancy Reiser M.Ed, the wife of Dr. David E. Reiser M.D., the long-ago psychiatrist/psychoanalyst who took me with him when he talked to the Fire Setter, counsels the siblings of autistic children, helping them to come to terms with their distress. She has a waist high, tabletop sand box, beside it a bookcase stuffed with every sort and kind of dollhouse figure, furniture, tree, bush, and pet. She tells her children they can play with all of it and make up scenes if they want to. Often children play out scenes of anguish.

"Sometimes," Nancy says, "I take these two arm chairs and turn them on their side and throw a blanket over them. Like this, see? It makes a little cave a child can creep into. Sometimes, I offer her a lamp to take in with her. Then I knock on the door and ask if I may come in. I only come in if I'm invited."

Often siblings confide to Nancy what they can't bear to tell their own mother, for fear of hurting her feelings.

Nancy, sensing my elderly distress at this, says, "Every child should have two mothers. Lots of children need a 'second mother,' another adult who can listen and understand when their own mothers are burdened."

My own feeling history?

I look back on the early years of raising Temple, those years when I hid and denied my feelings, and recognize today how my denial contributed to my inadequacy. But then I wonder if I could have survived without that denial? It gave me time to make room for hope—real hope, not Hallmark Card hope. Hope born of knowing the options and actively taking them on, that's what brings nurture into play.*

---

* Jerome Groopman, M.D., *The Anatomy of Hope*, Random House, 2004.

At every autism lecture today I meet denying parents and I wouldn't want to rob them of that first reaction. I see my young self in them, and remember—while my young self was stalling around denying—my extraordinary good luck. Not brains, not insight, no so-called courage. Just plain old "good luck." I pray a little comes their way. And along with the luck, some extra money. At a time when I needed it, I had money.

Today, listening to the parents' stories, I remember the Leave-it-to-Beaver world. I'll always be grateful for the kind, protective haven it provided for Temple. But today I can see, along with all its good points, its limitations and denials. After I was divorced, my telephone rang only four times between Labor Day and Christmas. The first was for my Boston Symphony ticket. Permanent Friday afternoon Symphony seats were hard to come by in those days. The second was for the Irish girls. Good baby sitters were hard to come by, too. The third call was for my vote, and the fourth for my blood. I then remember, with a certain grim amusement, a neighbor's outrage that I was at Harvard. Her son was the first in a long line of Harvard men not to be accepted as an undergraduate. She became convinced I was taking up his space.

It was a charming world, that Leave-it-to-Beaver world, one that I still miss, but one that never would have been suitable for Temple as an adult. I, too, had to leave. The feeling part of me couldn't accept it for a lifetime identity. With a certain wistful sorrow, I've shed it and left it behind—an old snake skin, blowing away in the grass.

And Dick? What about his feeling history?

The idea that all existence, whatever its patterns, is essentially fluid and subject to change, was too threatening a notion for Dick even to contemplate. If nothing is fixed, then what was the point to the golden world he'd been born into? In the end, desperate to keep his life in a holding pattern, Dick saw my shifting choices for Temple and for myself as insane. It wasn't an angry divorce maneuver but a deeply felt battle to defend his world from change.

And what a beautiful world it was—that life Dick introduced me to, all those years ago when I was a bride—its graceful patterns stretching back over the generations. The old family apartment in Boston, with the crackle of starched aprons as the maids circled the dining table. The summer house on the Vineyard with every room looking out on the dazzling blue Sound. The Sound lulling him to sleep at night with the soft slurp of its inland tide, the tip of each ripple bright with moonlight.

And parties on porches, with flowery women and men in red linen pants, my father-in-law tucking a bachelor's button in his button hole, and sallying forth to joke with old friends. Tennis in the day and dance music on Saturday night. That's what Dick dreamed of in the heat of WWII. He didn't think of his life as privileged. He thought of it as home.

Then suddenly, unbearably, home was savaged. Autism was an appalling enemy. If I couldn't see that, then I, too, must be the enemy. His obsession grew monstrous; he went to battle to destroy us for our own good and, in the end, it led him to dedicating his life to proving God didn't exist.

Yet, through it all, he never lost his faith in the stock market. At night he would lull himself to sleep, adding up figures from the financial page, writing them down in long columns on the flyleaf of whatever book was handy. To this day I still open books and find those deeply incised columns of calculation. Reliable, enduring.

Whereas God, like a young dogwood, might not make it through the winter.

Before he died, Dick left word that his body was to be given to a medical school, not so much for the edification of medics but to prevent a Christian burial. But burial ceremonies are for the living. After the medics had finished with his invaded body, his children laid his ashes to rest in Mt. Auburn Cemetery in Cambridge.

I remember, when I was a child, how the oculist used a dense black velvet cloth to graph my ocular blind spot. He told me to stare at the white dot in the center of the velvet, while he moved a silver pencil across it.

"Tell me when you can no longer see the pencil; then tell me when it appears again." Each time I told him, he'd put a pin into the velvet. Again and again, until, suddenly, the pins had formed a circle.

"There," the oculist said. "That's your blind spot." But the blind spot wasn't on the velvet; it was in me.

It's taken me all these years to understand that the rigidity, the tension, the temper, the obsession—the traits Dick so despised in his daughter—they were all his own. And who was there to help him in his childhood, long before anyone had coined the word "autism?"

Now at last I see it. My rage is gone; sorrow hits, and I ache to forgive.

Fifty years ago, Anthropologist and Naturalist Loren Eiseley wrote about the extraordinary change that took place in us, back in the lost eons of man's early human development.

He was becoming something the world had never seen before—
a dream animal—living at least partially within a secret uni-
verse of his own creation and sharing that secret universe in his
head with other, similar heads. Symbolic communication had
begun. Man had escaped from the eternal present of the animal

world into a knowledge of past and future. The unseen gods, the powers behind the world of phenomenal appearance, began to stalk through his dreams. *

When you look at it that way, yes, we're dream creatures. Even our alphabet is a dream. Twenty-six little symbols we put together in different combinations to say the words that express our feelings. Here on these pages I've arranged those words to conjure up what is no longer a phenomenal reality, but a memory dream. And this kind of conjure with its inferences, its contradictions and ironies, is deeply puzzling to people with autism. Theirs is a painting-by-numbers world, recognizable, but never quite the real thing. It's the "never quite" that makes autism such an unsettling disorder.

The other night I went to see *Big River*, a musical version of Mark Twain's *Huckleberry Finn*. Half of the cast was made up of actors from the Theatre of the Deaf, and the other half were hearing actors. The hearing sang for the deaf; the deaf, who can lip read, lip synched. Everybody "signed." The singing, the synching, and the signing were so effective that it took a little time to catch onto who was actually singing and who couldn't hear the music.

Suddenly, all music, song and sound cut off, and there was utter silence. Unaware of it, the cast went right on synching and signing. The audience watched, stunned. The deaf actors were so good at our hearing world that we'd forgotten it wasn't theirs, that the kid playing Huck was dancing, not to the music, but to the vibration of the stage floor.

Like autism, total deafness is a world unto itself.

In spite of Temple's conviction that she has no feelings, that she relies on reason and logic alone, Temple does have her dream

---

* Loren Eisley, *The Immense Journey*, Vintage, 1946.

side. In particular her "little door" dream, which goes all the way back to her years at Hampshire Country School. Autistic young people, if you remember, have trouble with prepositions; that is, until they've experienced them literally.

There was a little construction door in Temple's school dormitory that led to the roof. When she finally dared to step "through" it, she found she was actually out on the sloping roof, a bit unnerved by the height but deeply moved by the starry night sky. From that night on, "going through the little door" became Temple's symbolic act of preparation for the next step in life. Even now, she walks herself through various doors. Today I'm astonished by Temple's worldly accomplishments, but what I love most about her is her courage. Despite the hazards of her autistic landscape, she's never hesitated to go "through the little door," with no guarantee that what's on the other side will ever make sense to her.

Temple's other dream—perhaps her most intense one—is of cows in their final step. She takes great pride in her slaughter construction, a design of her own that conducts them to a painless oblivion. She calls it her stairway to heaven and gets down in the walkway herself so she can identify with the cows as they amble, one behind the other, unaware of the moment ahead that will turn them from living creatures into meat.

Has Temple changed me? Yes, of course, and continues to. After conferences, we often have dinner together and share our adventures. Despite her extraordinary accomplishments, she knows that some part of the dream that I call "life" lies a little beyond her. It accounts for her hunger to have me understand *her* dream: that she won't be forgotten. Her longing for some kind of permanent recognition is so palpably real, she moves me deeply with it.

As if love were too mysterious and shaky to rely on.

Yet despite her insistence that she will never know what love is, I see that what I've said about her father at our joint autism conference weighs deeply on her.

"I know what you think of Daddy," she says as she buys herself a *Wall Street Journal* in the airport where we're waiting to fly away from each other. "But he sent me the *Wall Street Journal* every day I was in boarding school. And I still read it."

Whatever she thinks she feels or doesn't feel, she holds on tight to that precious connection.

But Temple is only one of my children. I've told how doctors, therapists, teachers and neighbors helped Temple but not how the siblings helped her. I've shared my difficulties with Dick, but not those the siblings had to suffer, both when they were little and after Dick and I were divorced. Young or adult, whenever the year or whatever the place, the siblings always protected Temple from her father.

Yes, Temple's changed me, but the siblings, with their generous laughter, their talent and warmth, have also changed me. I've held to my promise in that I've kept their role in this story intentionally vague, but they are not vague.

All four children lie at the heart of my feeling brain.

Nonfiction

Thomas Cahill, *How the Irish Saved Civilization: The Untold Story of Ireland's Heroic Role from the Fall of Rome to the Rise of Medieval Europe.* Doubleday, NY, 1995.
First vol. Of Cahill's series, *The Hinges of History.* Recounts how the Irish monks preserved Greek and early Christian manuscripts after the fall of Rome. Conveys the constantly shifting flow of the human thought. If you read nothing else, read the pages on "shape shifting."

Frank Close, *Lucifer's Legacy: The Meaning of Asymmetry.* Oxford University Press, NY, 2000.
Probes the lopsidedness of all life. Helpful in understanding the sidedness of autism.

Antonio R. Damasio, *Descartes Error: Emotion, Reason and the Human Brain.* Avon Books, Inc., NYC, 1994.

Antonio R. Damasio, *The Feeling of What Happens: Body and Emotion in the Making of Consciousness.* Harcourt Brace, 1999.
Both Damasio books explore the neurological links between emotion and thought.

The Editors of *Scientific American Magazine*, "Introduction" by Antonio R. Damasio, *The Scientific American Book on the Brain, The Best Writing on Consciousness, I.Q. and Intelligence, Perception, Disorders of the Mind.* The Lyon Press, 1999.
Contains an article on autism by Uta Frith.

Loren Eiseley, *The Immense Journey: an imaginative naturalist explores the mysteries of man and nature.* Vintage, 1946.
The slow, miraculous evolution of human sensibility.

Stephen Eliot, *Not the Thing I Was: Thirteen Years of Bruno Bettelheim's Orthogenic School.* St. Martin's Press, 2002.
Author with autism makes Bettelheim seem a little less of a monster; nevertheless, still a monster.

Erik H. Erikson, *Childhood and Society*, Norton, 1950.

Erik H. Erikson, *Insight and Responsibility: Lectures on the Ethical Implication of Psychoanalytic Insight.* Norton, 1964.
Erikson coined the word "identity," defining it as both the product and the determinant of society.

Barry Gordon, M.D., Ph.D. and Lisa Berger, *Intelligent Memory: *Increase productivity* Solve everyday problems faster* Learn to be more creative.* Viking, 2003.
Dr. Gordon forces you to take note of your mental process. A great read for you and that smart Asperger's child.

Temple Grandin and Margaret M. Scariano, *Emergence: Labeled Autistic.* Warner Books, 1986.

Temple Grandin, *Thinking in Pictures: and other reports from my life with Autism.* Vintage, NY, 1995.
Both books are tops on insight into the autistic mind.

Jerome Groopman, M.D., *The Anatomy of Hope: How People Prevail in the Face of Illness.* Random House, NY, 2004.
Writing of the age-old battle with illness and pain, Dr. Groopman includes his own experience.

Beth Kephart, *A Slant of Sun: One Child's Courage*, Norton, NY 1998.
A touching story of a mother of an autistic child.

Bibliography

Clara Claiborne Park, *The Seige: A Family's Journey into the World of an Autistic Child,* Little Brown, Boston, 1967.

Clara Claiborne Park, *Exciting Nirvana: A Daughter's Life with Autism,* Foreword by Oliver Sacks, Little Brown, 2001.
Two meticulously recorded stories of raising a daughter with autism. You won't forget either one.

Candace B. Pert, Ph.D., *Molecules of Emotion: Why You Feel the Way You Feel,* Foreword by Deepak Chopra, M.D., Scribner, 1997.
Covering some of the same ground as Damasio, Pert also tells her own life journey. Immensely readable.

Richard Pollack, *The Creation of Dr.B: A Biography of Bruno Bettelheim,* Simon & Schuster, NY, 1997.
Read it!

Dawn Prince-Highes, editor, *Aquamarine Blue 5: Personal Stories of College Students with Autism.* Ohio University Press, Ohio, 2002.
Five absorbing stories edited by Prince-Hughes, who also has autism.

V.S. Ramachandran. M.D, Ph.D. and Sandra Blakeslee, Forward by Oliver Sacks, *Phantoms in the Brain: Probing the Mysteries of the Human Mind.* Quill/William Morrow, Harper Collins, NY, 1998.
Think you're constant and consistent? Think again.

Richard Restak, M.D., *The Secret Life of the Brain.* Joseph Henry Press, National Academy Press, Washington, D.C.
Based on the public television program on the brain.

Matt Ridley, *Nature Via Nurture: Genes, Experience & What Makes Us Human,* Harper Collins, NY, 2003.

Our genes are not merely "the implacable little determin-
ists" we thought they were, but "the mechanism for experience".

Oliver Sacks, *An Anthropologist on Mars: Seven Paradoxical Tales*,
Vintage Books, Random House, NY, 1995.
Sacks' tales include his account of Temple Grandin.

C.P. Snow, *The Two Cultures and the Scientific Revolution*,
Cambridge University Press, NY, 1961.
Snow's book, impacted the sixties.

Plays and Fiction

T.S. Eliot, *The Family Reunion: A Verse Play with a Contemporary
Setting*, Harcourt Brace, NY, copyright 1939
The play that determined my life.

Michael Frayn, *Copenhagen: Methuen Drama*, UK, 1998
"The Whole possibility of saying or thinking anything about
the world, even the most apparently objective, abstract
aspect of it studied by the natural sciences, depends upon
human observation, and is subject to the limitations which
the human mind imposes, this uncertainty in our thinking
is also fundamental to the nature of the world."
Excerpted from Frayn's "postscript" to his play.

Mark Haddon, *The Curious Incident of the Dog in the Nighttime*.
Vintage Contemporaries, 2004.
Fifteen-year-old boy with autism sets out to unravel the
mysterious death of his neighbor's poodle. Enchanting
page-turner.

Henry James, *The Turn of the Screw and Other Short Fiction*.

Bantom Books, 1981. Copyright Scribner, 1908
Still the best ghost story ever written.

Archibald MacLeish, *Herakles, a play in verse.* Houghton
Mifflin, Boston, 1964
The hubris of power seen through the ancient Greek myth.

Bram Stoker, *Dracula*, Penguin, 1994. First published, 1897

Richard Wilbur, *The Misanthrope and Tartuffe: Moière Translated
into English Verse by Wilbur*, Harcourt Brace, first copyright,
1954.
"Here is a new master of translation's difficult art." *The
New Yorker*

A Few Organization References

Autism Research Institute, 4182 Adams Avenue, San Diego, CA
92116. Bernard Rimland, Ph.D., Director.

Autism Research Program at the University of Pittsburgh
Medical Center, Webster Hall, Suite 300, 3811 O'Hara Street,
Pittsburgh, PA 15213. Nancy Minshaw, M.D., Director.

Autism Services Center, P.O. Box 507, Huntington, WV 25710-
0507. Phone: (304) 525-8014 Fax: (304) 525-8026. Ruth
Christ Sullivan, Ph.D., Director.
Provides life-long, comprehensive, community based servic-
es to individuals with developmental disabilities.
Specializing in autism.

FHautism.com, 721 W. Abram St., Arlington, TX 76013.
Phone: (800) 489-0727. Jennifer Gilpin Yacio, President.
The world leader in publications and conferences on autism
and Asperger's.

Seaver & New York Autism Center of Excellence, Mount Sinai School of Medicine, NYC. Eric Hollander, M.D. Director.
New insights in the diagnosis, neurobiology, genetics, and treatment of autism.

TEACCH, Department of Psychiatry, School of Medicine, University of North Carolina at Chapel Hill. NC., Gary Mesibov Ph.D., Director.
Treatment and education of autistic and related communication-handicapped children. Also an international, interdisciplinary center for research, service, and training.

University of Michigan Autism and Communication Disorder Center, (UMACC). 111 East Catherine Street, Ann Arbor, MI 48109. Catherine Lord, Ph.D., Director.

The Watson Institute, Sewickley, PA. Marilyn Hoyson, Ph.D., Director.
Educational organization specializing in the education of children with special needs; also in the education of the professionals and pre-professionals who serve them. Watson's web site, an interactive service, will answer questions addressed to: www.thewatsoninstitute.org .

About the Author

A Thorn in My Pocket is Eustacia Cutler's story of raising her autistic daughter, Temple Grandin, in the conservative "Leave-it-to-Beaver" world of the fifties, a time when autistic children were routinely diagnosed as "infant schizophrenics" and banished to institutions. She tells of her fight to keep Temple in the mainstream of family, community and school life, how Temple responded and went on to succeed, as Ms. Cutler puts it, "beyond my wildest dreams." Ms. Cutler also explores the nature of the autism disorder as doctors understand it today, and how its predominant characteristics reflect our own traits in an exaggerated form. A graduate of Harvard, Eustacia Cutler's lectures, aimed at helping mothers to deal with the unsettling effect of autism on the family identity, are well known in this country, Canada, Hong Kong and the U.K. She is also the mother of three other children, all younger than Temple.

Printed in the USA
CPSIA information can be obtained
at www.ICGtesting.com
JSHW011418220324
59659JS00002B/3

9 781941 765401